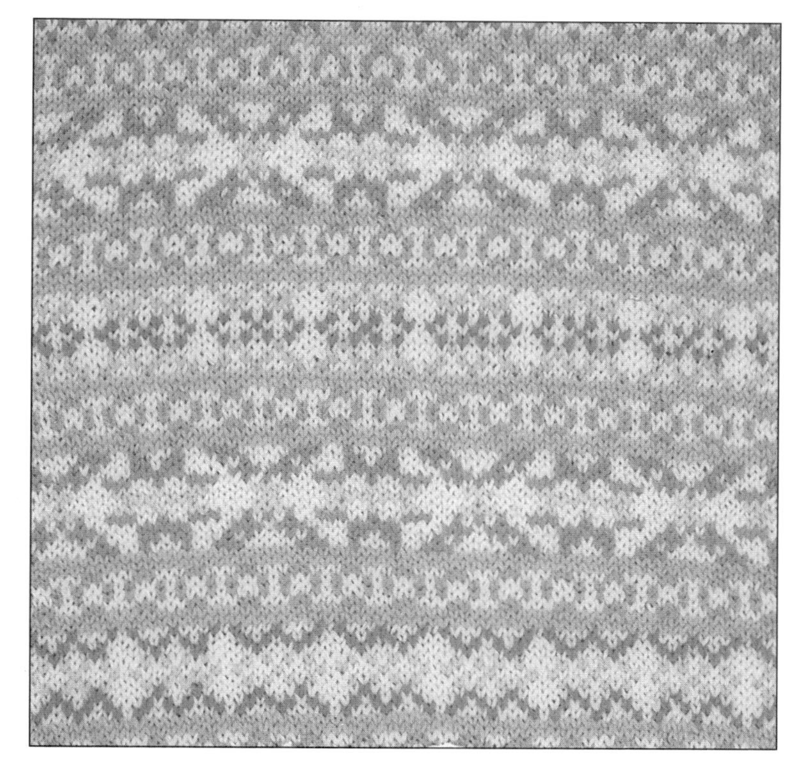

Fabulous

Fairisle

JOHN ALLEN

LOCHAR PUBLISHING · MOFFAT · SCOTLAND

To the Knitters of Scotland.

ACKNOWLEDGEMENTS

MANY THANKS TO Middlesex Polytechnic who awarded me a bursary to assist in the expenses incurred in researching the book. I wish to thank the following friends for all their help and assistance, Ted Houghton and Heather Stuart, who worked with me in my studio. Lilian Dodds and Jon Crane for their support and encouragement, and Margaret Stuart, Hazel Hughson, Wilma Malcolmson and Jean Harlcrow, all of whom allowed me to feature them and their work in this book. Jean and Wilma also were responsible for writing the patterns and producing the machine knitted garments and some of the swatches and kept me company burning the midnight oil! Thanks to Elspeth Sinclair for assisting in the knitting of some of the hand knitted swatches and thanks to Rosella Downie for writing the patterns for the hand knitted sweaters, knitting them and for all her other help and assistance. I also wish to thank the Tourist Office in Lerwick and the Lerwick Museum and all the staff in both organisations who made me so welcome during my stay in Shetland and offered me every assistance possible, many thanks also to the authorities of both establishments for allowing me to reproduce here some of the photographs from their archives. Finally, thanks to Debbie Hatley whose sketches accompany the garment patterns and which illustrate the last section of the book. Without the help and support of all these very generous people this book could not have been possible.

Published by Lochar Publishing Ltd
Moffat DG10 9JU

Designed by Hammond Hammond

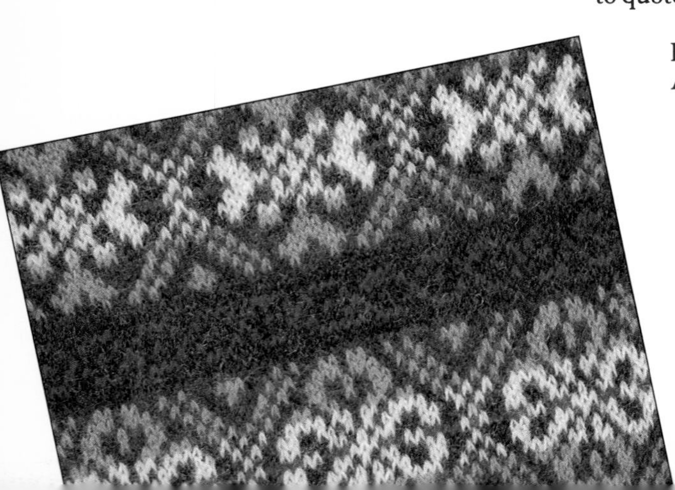

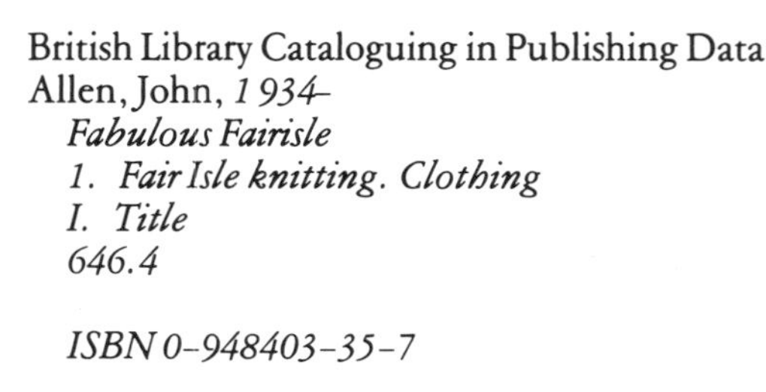

British Library Cataloguing in Publishing Data
Allen, John, *1934–*
Fabulous Fairisle
1. Fair Isle knitting. Clothing
I. Title
646.4

ISBN 0-948403-35-7

The photographs on pages 2 and 3 are: Ronas Voe (far left), the island of Fairisle (left) and Weisdale Kirk on Shetland (right).

Contents

Introduction

THIS BOOK WILL appeal to all people interested in pattern and design, as well as knitters. It can be used as a source book for ideas, something that can be dipped into and used for reference, not just read once and relegated to the shelf. To this end, the major part of the book is given over to the patterns and their manipulations. The Island of Fair Isle, usually a prominent feature in any book of fairisle knitting, plays little part here. Instead, I shall concentrate on Shetland (the majority of the knitters carrying on the tradition of classic fairisle knitting live on this the main island), the island's knitters, and on the contemporary knitting of fairisle, experimenting with the patterns and illustrating many of the different uses these can be put to in designs.

How did these fabulous fairisle patterns come into being? Who invented the structures on which these patterns are made? Where and how are the wonderful coloured and elaborately patterned sweaters now produced, and by whom? I hope in this book not only to answer these questions, but to inspire the reader to go away and begin to create his or her own fairisle patterns and sweaters, by giving examples of traditional and innovative ways of working with fairisle.

Knitting is practised by an ever-growing number of people, it is estimated to be some 7,000,000 at the present time and this number is continually expanding. In the past, men dominated the craft, but during this century the tables have been turned for social and economic reasons. Nowadays, the man who knits is the exception and the woman dominates.

At present, knitting is created for pleasure and is a major hobby. Indeed, one could say an industry. The demands of the home knitter keep many mills and manufacturers extremely busy producing the essential artifacts necessary to knit – needles, yarns, and patterns – but this has not always been the case. Not long ago knitting was an essential part of any family's income. This in itself is a fascinating story, but it is not my intention to write a social history of knitting. This book presents fairisle knitting as I have come to see and appreciate it while working over the last eight years among the professional knitters on the Shetland Islands. I have visited the main islands regularly and have been privileged to become friends with many of the Shetland knitters, seeing at first hand their skills and talents. Watching each knitter bring their own talents to these classic patterns giving them their individual, distinctive styles. I want not only to show a little of the great richness of fairisle, but also describe and illustrate something of the background of some of the designer/knitters working today on Shetland.

I have always been fascinated by the present-day islanders' approach to knitting and the way they manipulate the patterns. It is intriguing to observe how the colours are selected and worked into the knitting to create the wonderful combinations we all so enjoy wearing. Some years ago I was asked to design a small range of fairisle sweaters for a company on the island and discovered, first-hand, how complex the colouring of the patterns is. I discovered that it took longer sometimes to get the right colour combination, than to originate the pattern sequence or even the sweater style! The knitters on the island, mostly untrained, work such combinations out as though it were second nature.

To really appreciate fairisle knitting and understand its evolution it is important to know a little about the history and the environment it is produced in. This book starts with a look at these two important aspects, conjuring up by the use of photographs something of the wild, rugged, but always beautiful, landscape, which so influences the knitters' use of colour.

The design section then begins with a glossary of illustrations of traditional patterns. I have included as many of these as was practicable and to my knowledge for the first time many of these are shown in knitted form alongside the usual graphs, to enable the knitter to visualize them more easily. From the single patterns, I illustrate the manipulation and development of these into repeating patterns, which can be used directly in sweaters.

It is my intention to encourage the knitter to consider designing his or her own repeating patterns and I explain how to achieve this, by illustrating ways to exploit fairisle patterns and showing original ideas by which the reader can achieve exciting results. Sweater patterns in classic styles for both hand and machine knitters are also included. Ways are shown by which any of the patterns illustrated in the book can be superimposed upon any of the sweater styles, thus creating a whole pattern book of designs from which any reasonably competent machine or hand knitter can work to produce their own exciting designs.

I hope that by writing this book and showing some of the wonderful patterns available I will inspire knitters to try out their own original ideas and that the book will encourage a more original approach to the knitting craft.

John Allen

Sweater, scarf and hat in the collection of the Shetland Museum.

CHAPTER ONE

A History

IT IS NOT within the remit of this book to provide a general history of knitting, but some facts about the development of the craft are relevant in helping us to understand the art and set the history of fairisle knitting into perspective. The history of the development of fairisle knitting is complex, it is also compounded by the many different theories put forward as to where the patterns used in the knitting originated, and any hard facts until the mid-nineteenth century are difficult to find. The numerous books written on the subject give conflicting views and accounts. Facts and myths become almost indistinguishable, just as in any good detective story, but the end of this story, reveals that there are still elements of the mystery to be unravelled.

It is known that knitting was a highly advanced craft in Egypt as early as the fourth century BC and at the other side of the world, Peruvian knitting goes back to the third century BC. There are examples of such knitting in museums, and it is generally thought that from these two great civilizations knitting originated and eventually spread through the then known world. The Egyptians were highly civilized at that period, and were also great traders known to have ventured long distances outside the Mediterranean. Likewise, the Peruvians, whose crafts skills are well documented, were cruelly conquered by the Spaniards, so allowing their cultural influences to spread to Europe, although this was centuries later. From these few facts, one can begin to see the complexities of pin pointing the originator of specific design forms related to the knitting craft.

Scarfs, and a sweater from the historical collection of Fairisle in the Shetland Museum.

There is no evidence as to when two-colour knitting evolved, or even when knitting graduated onto two needles from the one, which most early knitting techniques required. Certainly by the twelfth century the Arabs around the Mediterranean had developed two-colour knitting on two needles. At this time, the Arabs were highly skilled in many of the crafts and great traders, so it would be easy for the two-colour knitting they had developed to be passed on as they extended their influence around Europe. At least here we have facts. It is known that the Arab rulers of Sicily influenced the weaving of silk brocade which was produced there, not only technically, but in the design and patterning. They also had a strong influence on all the countries they colonized, and there seems no reason why such a strong influence should not have been felt by people the Arabs also traded with. They and their culture were so different, even exotic to Europeans, it would have caused great interest.

COMBINED DEVELOPMENT

The development and spread of knitting must be seen alongside that of the evolution of other crafts, such as weaving, embroidery and tapestry. From what is known, the design and patterning of these was far in advance of that of knitting. In the case of weaving, the design and patterning was highly sophisticated by the twelfth century. It is certain that the patterns and designs used in these other crafts would have been seen and could not fail to influence crafts people involved in knitting. This is an interesting point, as there are definite similarities between fairisle patterning and some of the Sicillian and Spanish patterns used in Brocade-weaving at that time, although no link so far has been found. This theory must be viewed against events and

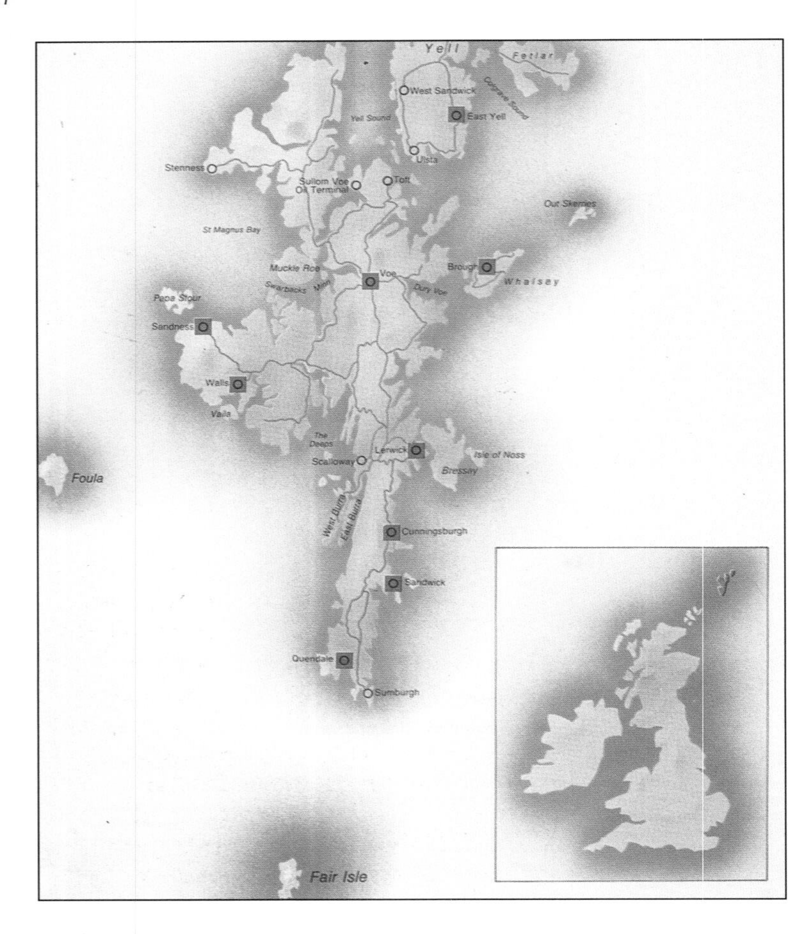

This map shows the major areas of conservation on Shetland and the insert illustration the island's position in relation to the mainland.

movements of people at that particular time. From 1200 to the Armada, trading was carried on between all the nations surrounding the Mediterranean, North Sea and Britain. Ambassadors moved from court to court, all bringing with them influences from their native countries; the cross-fertilization of ideas, designs and patterns must have taken place, and the evolution of these is continuous.

By the sixteenth century there were great Guilds formed in many countries and we know knitting was one of the crafts so governed. We also have examples of knitting from many countries from this period. The most popular use of knitting at this time was for knitted hose, particularly fashionable at the royal courts in Europe. The production of these is well documented and we know Queen Elizabeth I wore silk hose imported from Spain. There are examples of single colour knitting from this period in our museums and great country mansions like Hatfield House, but none of stranded (two colours in one row) knitting. The trade in imported silk hose was well established long before the British knitters could compete in quality. How the breakthrough came which allowed British knitting to compete with the fine silk imported hose is not known, but one story is that one William Riley saw a set of hose in an Italian merchant's house in London and borrowed these and copied them. As knitted hose was common at this time, we can only assume that he copied a technique, very possibly heel turning. Hose produced in Britain around this date had no heel fashioning, only the imported hose were fashioned to fit the foot as we know them today.

Even before Elizabeth, knitted hats, caps, gloves, sleeves and petticoats were knitted at the Tudor court. While France and Spain produced the finest silk hose, Britain had a reputation for knitted caps. In 1488, Henry VII tried to fix the price of English woollens (knitted caps) at two shillings. These caps remained fashionable for over a century and appear regularly in Tudor portraits, particularly those painted by Hans Holbein. In 1571, there was an Act of Parliament called the 'Cappers Act', decreeing that every gentleman below a certain rank had to wear a cap or pay a fine. Was this the start of the fashion for working men to wear caps?

SAILOR KNITTERS

In 1589, William Lee invented the knitting frame. But so much pressure was put on the Queen by the merchants and the hand-knitting industry that she was persuaded to ban its use. Unfortunately, like so many times since, the invention was handed over to be exploited and developed overseas. This event illustrates the strength of the knitting lobby and its importance. This happened one year after the Spanish Armada and the first stories of the originating of fairisle knitting on the island it is named after. The most popular story is of Spanish sailors shipwrecked on the rugged coast of Fair Isle after the defeat of the Armada. How these sailor knitters taught the island hosts the technique of two-colour knitting and showed them the patterns they knew is not known. Although there is historical proof that the unfortunate Duke of Medina, one Admiral Juan Gomez de Medine, and his crew were shipwrecked on the coast of Fair Isle, there is no evidence as to what really happened. However, another story goes that the islanders, frightened by this sudden increase in their numbers by unwelcome foreigners feared this might cause a famine, so they hid as much of their food and animals as was possible. The result of this was that many of the sailors died of starvation. The weak and wretched among the Spaniards were quickly finished off by the islanders. There are stories of them being thrown off cliffs back into the sea and worse. Certainly there must have been great problems, as the authorities on the main island of Shetland sent a boat to pick up the Duke of Medina and his surviving crew. The last part of this

Knitting Graphs for Latvian Mittens demonstrating the similarity between these patterns and those used in fairisle knitting.

story can be given some credence, as there is documentary evidence of the same Duke, wintering in Shetland before returning to Spain after being shipwrecked.

There were other opportunities for the Shetland knitters to learn from foreign sources. Bounty would certainly have been taken from the Armada wrecks, among which there could have been examples of two-colour knitting and strange patterns. We know the Spaniards had knitted accessories, such items if retrieved from the wrecks would be examined by the islanders and by this time the knitters there would have had the skill to copy them. It is interesting that as yet there is no mention of fairisle knitting made by any visitors to the islands. This did not occur until the mid-nineteenth century. This is odd indeed if these tales are true, and it is even stranger when one considers the distinctive colouring and patterning of fairisle knitting. Surely observant travellers recording their journeys would have noted such unique knitting if they had seen it?

Let us now continue with the general history, where there may be clues to help find out more about the origins of fairisle. In 1666 Samuel Pepys records in his diary that he wore a thin silk waistcoat, and the making up of this garment is described. There is continually more evidence coming to light on the knitting of this period, and certainly sophisticated silk Brocade knitting was being produced. By the eighteenth century, there were well-established knitting frame workshops, and Venetian frame knitters complained of unfair competition from the hand knitters! Only by producing silk shirts with patterns of great variety and richness could the hand frame knitters survive. Even so, throughout the eighteenth century knitting prospered. Aberdeen was exporting more than £100,000's worth of knitted stockings during this period, many produced in the Shetlands.

CHANGING FASHION

Changing times at the end of the century, linked with changing fashion, saw the demise of the stocking trade and great turmoil resulted in the knitting industry. The Aberdeen trade being directly linked to the Shetlands, its demise brought great hardship to the islands. It was this disaster which started the knitters on the main island of Shetland to start trading in lace knitting which had been evolving on the island for some time. This was developed and became the mainstay of knitters on the island and was still knitted in some quantity at the end of the last century. While the knitters on Shetland struggled to recover from the demise of the stocking trade and develop lace knitting, the first fairisle knitting is recorded being seen on the island of Fair Isle in 1851. The fairisle knitting seen is described as having strange, wonderful patterns in colours that dazzle. From this date, fairisle knitting is recorded and its development can be traced with some certainty.

In 1951, a man's body was found on the island of Fair Isle buried in a peat bog. Some fairisle knitting was found including the well-preserved knitted hose, gloves, cape and patterned purse. The purse contained coins dated 1681 and 1690! The problem is knowing whether this man was a trader, visitor or islander. What is does prove is that there was patterned knitting on the island of Fair Isle much earlier than the first recorded sighting of 1851. All manner of speculation has been opened up by this discovery.

Many of the theories and stories regarding the origins of fairisle patterns and knitting may not bear close examination. However, this does not mean that they have no grain of truth in them. There is no doubt that the fairisle patterns and knitting technique have a foreign source, and we know Shetland knitters certainly would have had contact with a wide variety of foreign people, seaborn from Europe. We also know the islanders had frequent traders from the countries round the Baltic and North seas visit them. The evolution of design styles in any form is usually a slow, complex and continuous process over many years and decades. Fairisle patterns and knitting can be no exception to this and the Shetland islands were uniquely situated for this to happen there.

A CROSSROADS

The Shetland Islands were owned by Norway until they were sold to Scotland in 1469. So there has to have been a strong Nordic cultural input into the islands at this early date. We also know that from 1610 to 1710 the Shetlanders held a fair in Lerwick, the capital of the islands. This fair was known abroad and visited by foreign ships, indeed the Reverend, George Lee on a visit in 1774 found over 400 vessels in Bressay Sound, the harbour of the main island. He goes on to say that 200 of these ships were Dutch and the remainder Prussian, French, Danish and Flemish. This demonstrates the importance of Shetland to foreign fleets and it was also a trading centre and cross roads for shipping. Far from being isolated, the Shetlands were and are very strategically placed to be a maritime trading centre, which is what they obviously were at this time. These trading ships brought textiles, spirits and grain to sell and barter in exchange for knitting.

It is recorded that the whole year's production of knitting would be sold or exchanged at the fair. But what kind of knitting was being produced which was so desirable to Europeans that they would travel so far to obtain it? Could it be just hose or lace? Could the first fairisle knitted items have been brought over from the island of Fair Isle to sell? Or could the Shetland knitters on the main island have been producing interesting two-colour knitting by this time? There are so many possibilities. The knitting traded certainly had to be different to what the foreigners themselves could produce.

So, on the Shetland islands there was a group of creative crafts people with a high level of perspective skills. They were constantly in contact with foreign people in their foreign clothes, made out of fabrics in patterns, strange and different to anything the islanders had previously experienced. Many of the countries round the Baltic and North seas had developed knitting traditions, which contained distinctive patterns and styles. It is interesting to look at just one of these, Latvia, a small country in the Eastern Baltic for many of the patterns used by the Latvian knitters are very similar to fairisle ones. The main difference is in the arrangement of the patterns, their repeating sequence and colour although single motifs are very similar to fairisle ones.

If the Shetland knitters saw such rich patterns, which they surely must have done, it would be surprising indeed if they were not influenced by them. They had plenty of opportunity to see other foreign travellers from Europe, many probably from southern Europe (the Spanish connection) with their Moorish influences. Given the mix of influences, it is easy to see how fairisle developed from humble beginnings to the richness of the patterns we know today. It would have been a natural progression, particularly among a creative craft-orientated community, which contained knitters with a higher than normal level of perceptive skills.

The first mechanical knitting machines were introduced onto the islands in the 1920s, and in the 1950s the first domestic hand frame knitting machines made by the Japanese appeared in the homes of some of the knitters. This was thought by many people to herald the end of hand knitting, but it has proved not to be the case. Certainly, hand knitting has declined, but there will always be knitters who work at the craft for its convenience, relaxing qualities and creative stimulation. This is increasingly true in a society where mass-produced products are becoming uniform. Today, hand knitting is still being produced of the highest order, admittedly in very small quantities, but the discerning can commission the one-off special sweater and be assured of receiving a small work of art.

With the setting up of the Shetland Trades Association in 1982, enormous developments have taken place in the organizing and production of knitting. It says much for the islands' knitters that they have worked the transition from hand craft to machine knitting so well and continue to produce knitting of such quality and in such glorious colours and patterns that the contemporary work has become an international classic, selling in many countries around the world, having universal appeal that still dazzles the eye.

Three sweaters and three hats in trhe Shetland Museum's historic collection of fairisle garments. These demonstrate the very different effects achieved by colour even in early examples of the knitting.

CHAPTER TWO

The Environment

IN THIS CHAPTER I shall concentrate on the Island of Shetland as its environment closely reflects that of the other islands in the group. It is often forgotten that the Shetlands consists of over 100 islands only a small number of which, something like sixteen, are inhabited. Shetland is about 180 miles from the coast of Norway and 200 miles from mainland Scotland. The island of Fair Isle is south of the main group and rather isolated, as can be seen from the map on page 10. If one did a drawing of the coast line what a fretwork jigsaw it would be. The sea seems to have shaped the land into every contortion possible and the shape of this, along with the voes (sea inlets), are one of the island's great scenic attractions.

People often refer to the Shetlands as being remote, even isolated. This is not strictly true today. The main island is accessible by large planes and ferries and Lerwick has one of Britain's greatest safe water harbours at Bressay Sound, spectacularly sheltered by the island of Bressay, from which the Sound gets its name. The harbour has been used throughout history as a safe haven and trading post. This was particularly so in World War II and is still used today, even though it is of less importance. The P & O Ferries now disgorge their loads of tourists regularly at the dock and in the fishing season the Russian fishing fleet is very much in evidence.

The distinctive-looking Shetland sheep.

ISLAND HOPPING

Until the 1930s, the islands relied on ferries for all transportation to and from mainland Scotland. Planes had landed on Shetland as early as 1931, but it was not until 1936 that a regular passenger service was started. Because of rivalry between two companies, Shetland was blessed with three return flights a day from the mainland. Unfortunately, this is not so today. There are two airfields on the main island. Tingwall which is 3 to 4 miles north of Lerwick and Sunbrugh which is located on the southern tip of Shetland, surrounded on three sides by sea. Sunbrugh has been continually expanded and developed since the Second World War and in the 1970s, with the discovery of oil off the coast of the Shetland Islands, a new, large terminal building was built. It was during this period that the airport was up-graded to accommodate larger modern planes. Tingwall has not been developed in this way and it is now used mainly for small planes, island hopping and domestic cargo.

If you fly into Shetland from the mainland, it is Sunbrugh you will fly into. From the southern tip of the main island high up in your plane you will get your first views of the countryside. These first glimpses of the landscape on a clear day are particularly beautiful. The coast line is seen to advantage, your height in the plane allowing spectacular views of its rugged rocky outline, broken by some of the most idyllic little bays and golden beaches imaginable. These would be a Mecca for the sun worshippers if only the island could guarantee a constant spell of sun and high temperatures, which perhaps thankfully it cannot. Looking north, the land can be seen rising, promising craggy hills, even mountains. The odd isolated croft or cottage is seen nestling close to the bays and a small fishing boat will probably be spied bobbing on the sea close to the shore. On a sunny day this approach and introduction to the Shetland landscape is quite magical. The first impressions on flying into Sunbrugh are an accurate guide to the scenery which awaits exploring.

On my first visit to Shetland I was quite unprepared for the variety of landscape on such a small island. I remember how strange it was to stand seeing for miles in all directions and not finding one tree. Then, one autumn I was there when the wind reached wild proportions, sweeping in from the sea across the peat moors and hills, taking one's breath away. I realised then why the few trees there on the islands are so extremely choosy as to where they grow. They huddle and nestle prudently round the crofts and farm buildings or other sheltered spots. When the Shetland winds have been experienced, total sympathy goes out to the trees. The few that have tried to grow in the open have been contorted by the wind and the struggle to survive has been so great that they are poor, bent, distorted specimens.

The landscape has altered little over the decades, except where man has sited modern installations for communication, defence and electricity. Even these, thankfully few, are dwarfed, swamped by the very surroundings they normally disrupt. There is something wonderfully majestic about the often bleak, but always haunting Shetland landscape. On a journey from the north to the south it is possible to drive through countryside of wonderful sweeping calm beauty, open rolling hills folding into each other, with the valleys filled by the voes, of which there are so many, and which give the Shetland landscape one of its most distinctive and beautiful features. They can pierce into the country for long distances. A few miles farther, and driving round the crest of a hill, one can suddenly be confronted by a coastal view with cliffs of forbidding proportions and colours, and wild restless seas pounding them relentlessly.

CHANGING LANDSCAPES

Driving further south, again the countryside is all changed. Here, one is surrounded by well worked peat moors running into grass enclosures, which roll gently down to the sea. It is usually in the latter landscape that the famous Shetland ponies can be seen. They are a picturesque feature against this backcloth of coast and sea, but they are reputed on the island to be rather spiteful of nature and prone to biting the unsuspecting! In all these changes of scene there are always to be seen the cottages, farms and crofts, dotted together forming little hamlets, but many still isolated, miles from their nearest neighbour. The buildings are mainly of grey stone or granite, rather severe in appearance with few frills of architectural niceties. They blend into the countryside and coast well, providing the tourist with romantic photographs of Shetland to take home. The whole Shetland landscape is one of contrasts, which echoes the constantly changeable weather and sea pounding the island on all sides. It is not to be wondered at that many of the fairisle knitters' use of colour is influenced by the environment they live in.

The light on Shetland is unusual and extraordinarily clear, it has a crispness which affects the perception of colour enormously. The other extreme is that sometimes for many days, even weeks, there can be a grey haze of sea mists and poor visibility. So not only do the knitters live in an inspiring varied landscape, seeing the colours of this change by the season, they also experience the rapid unpredictable changes in the weather which affect the light and colouring also. All this heightens the effects on colour and its perception. It is hard to imagine the sometimes rapid and extreme changes of colour in the landscape caused by the weather without having experienced it.

Bressay Sound surrounded by snow-covered hills on a clear sunny day with crystal blue skies can be quite magical. This is not because of its beauty, for there are many places of far greater beauty, but because of the light and the way this brings things into focus. The effect the light has, reflecting from the sea to the land and back to the sky, is very special. Painters often talk about the light at St Ives in Cornwall, many going there especially to paint by it. I believe Shetland has such light also, less consistently than in St Ives, but anyone with a sensitive eye to colour would recognise this and be inspired by the effects that it has on the colour in the landscape.

Living in such a varied environment, the canny Shetlanders have selected well where to live and many small hamlets nestle along the sides of the voes and the prettiest of the bays. The small towns are also established in beautiful spots, in particular Scalloway with its romantic ruined castle. Lerwick the capital, as one would expect, reserves for itself one of the most desirable locations. In front of the town is a stretch of sea providing a deep water bay protected by Bressay Island. On either side of the town are large bays with wonderful views, especially looking south. Behind the town are hills and peat moors, together providing a

A Shetland croft at Whiteness

Two views of Lerwick from the harbour – the weather giving an impressive demonstration of its influence on the colour of the surrounding scenery.

perfect setting, which through the changing seasons provide a constant inspiration for colouring.

The town is built mainly in grey stone and granite, which gives the town a cold look in winter, and which glistens in the summer sun. There are one or two interesting old buildings, but the town is mainly built in the Victoria style. Architecturally, the town is no more interesting than many others in Britain, but what makes it of particular interest and sets it apart, is its setting and the quaint old arrangement of the streets and alleyways called lanes. These run at right angles to each other and the arrangement has hardly been altered since 1896. The lanes are often no more than narrow passages running away from the sea up the hillsides between the shops and houses, often very steep and stepped. It is easy to imagine Lerwick at the turn of the century. The street names have a history all of their own, names such as Charlotte Lane, Fox Lane, Mariners Court, Pirate Lane and Mouthooley Street. Time spent meandering round Lerwick is always interesting, but beware of wandering eyes, so easily drawn to the many shops displaying the products of the Shetland knitters, which have made the island famous.

The Shetlands are also famous for their brochs. A broch is a circular fortress built entirely without mortar in local stone commonly known as Picts houses. It is now certain that these were built during the Iron Age and are regarded as the highest development of this type of building in Western Europe. The Shetlands boast ninety brochs and the one on the island of Mousa, just a few hundred yards off the coast of Shetland is the best preserved in Britain. The buildings are impressive structures, with walls of great thickness rising to over 40 feet. Most brochs in the Shetlands are situated along the shores and they are quite unique, like so much else in the Shetland environment. No modern day designer knitter could fail to be uninspired by them, both for the patterns and the stone forms in the buildings and the colour of the local stone when seen used in this way.

Shetland is renowned for its wild life; the island is like a huge nature reserve and is particularly blessed with a great abundance and variety of bird life. While the pleasures of bird watching on the island today are many, it was not always so. In the past, much superstition surrounded any unusual bird and often the sighting of such a bird brought terror to the local people who regarded them as omens of disaster. The cry of the Corncrake was regarded as a death call. Many parts of the island are named after birds. In earlier times, many of the islanders relied on the sea birds as a source of food. In the spring, eggs were gathered and the young birds eaten, while adult birds were fair game all the year round. The sea, like the land, also yields up a large variety of living things. Fish have always been plentiful, providing the islanders with food. Seals and otters are native to Shetland, whales can still sometimes be seen, but are a much rarer sight these days than in the past, when they were regularly driven ashore and killed. There is an old photograph of 1903 in Lerwick museum, which bears dreadful witness to the slaughter of whales that often took place.

The environment, like most things, has two sides. It gives a great deal but it also demands. The weather can be so extreme that even today Shetland can be cut off from the mainland and life for the farmers and those employed on the sea is never easy. The Gulf Stream acts as a great protector, stopping the island becoming totally snowbound for any length of time or, like its northern neighbours, frozen for months every winter. Nevertheless, the island's weather is always unpredictable.

Whatever the weather, the Shetland sheep seem to be around. These are hardy creatures, living out throughout the year and seemingly in every place. No matter where one scrambles, there will be sheep. They are not a particularly beautiful animal, but their fleece has produced wool which has become world famous. Like the sheep, the yarn produced from its wool is a hard-wearing fibre. The colour of the sheep is interesting; many black ones mix with every shade of grey and brown imaginable. It is from these mixers that the famous natural Shetland colours come.

There is little doubt that the knitters on the Shetlands have been and are influenced by the colours surrounding them, giving much of the present day knitting extremely distinguished colourings, which bear little relationship to the historical colourings of the past. Many have been inspired by the colours in their environment: the colours of the heather-covered hill in autumn, the peat banks, and the greens of the fields and hills are all great favourites. Put the natural colours obtained directly off the sheep alongside the historical colourings to be seen on the old historical pieces of knitting in Lerwick museum and you have a sensational palette to work from. More will be said about this in the design section.

Today, the environment of the Shetlanders will be seen by many to be idyllic, a pace of life all of its own, totally cut off from the pressures of the mainland yet enjoying all the modern comforts of life. An ideal situation, given its history, for the craft of fairisle knitting to blossom and grow into a cottage industry and a major generator of wealth for the island's economy of today.

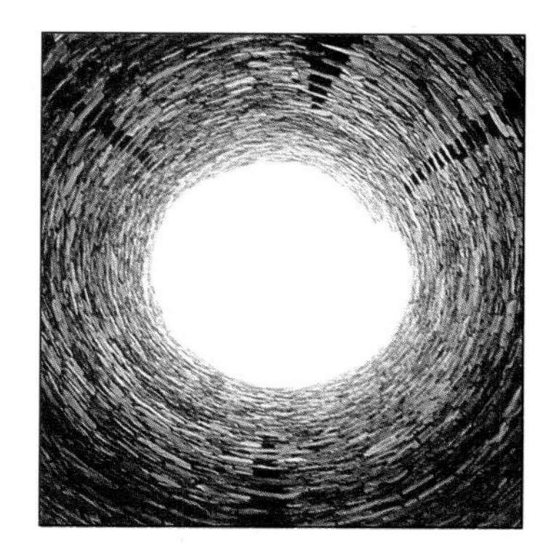

Mousa Broch and details taken from inside.

CHAPTER THREE

The Knitters

WITH ALL CRAFTS it is always difficult, if not impossible, to ascertain when developments happened or by whom they were initiated. The allover fairisle sweater is one such example for there is no evidence of one of these before around 1900. The first which did appear was a seamless garment knitted in the round. Whether this was on a circular needle or a set of needles is also a mystery. The sleeves are knitted down from the shoulders which to many knitters on mainland Britain is unusual, But this is the traditional method and quite common on the Shetlands among hand knitters, even today. Circular knitting allows the garment to be made without seams or any bad joins in the patterns. The finish of these hand knitted garments was, and is, always immaculate. While these sweaters can still be commissioned, less and less are available, mainly because of the hours of work involved and reluctance on the part of customers to accept this when reflected in the price. A beautiful hand-knitted fairisle sweater using the traditional methods is a work of art and is something still not properly appreciated by the public. It is interesting when looking at the historical collection of fairisle knitting in Lerwick Museum to note that many of the earlier sweaters were not so beautifully finished as some of the modern day ones. The reason for this is that most early sweaters were knitted as working garments, every day wear for the crofters and fishermen. Only later, when the sweaters began to be worn for pleasure and leisure, did the finish of the garment and knitting become so important that great attention was paid to it.

ROYAL APPROVAL

It is not known when the first allover fairisle sweaters appeared on the market, but they must have been available for sometime before 1921. In that year, it is recorded that Mr James Smith, a draper, presented a fairisle sweater to the Prince of Wales (later Edward VII). The present was obviously much appreciated, as we know the Prince wore it on the golf course at St Andrews that same year. Later, Sir Henry Lander painted the Prince's portrait and this shows him wearing the fairisle sweater again. In those days, even more than today, royal patronage could and did set fashions. The Prince's wearing of the fairisle sweater set a fashion among the young undergraduates in England and this popularized fairisle, setting a trend. Since this time, fairisle has been in and out of fashion many times, but it has always remained a firm favourite in the traditional styles of crew and vee necks: it is now a classic garment worldwide.

NATURAL DYES

It is not my intention to write about the knitters of bygone times for this has already been covered in other books, but a few details about them will enable us to appreciate the great steps forward which have taken place more recently. The photographs of some of the early knitters and their customers which can be seen in the Lerwick Museum are fascinating, those reprinted here give wonderful pictorial insights into the ways the sweaters were worn and the knitters who made them. In the museum, there are also documents which relate to the knitters, and one pattern note book illustrating how patterns were worked out. It seems a pity that no one has written a detailed social history about how the craft was developed and kept alive. Among the photographs in the Museum there are many of groups of women knitting in different surroundings; also of groups carding and spinning inside and outside their homes. We know that knitting was produced to earn money and many of the knitters used to take their sweaters to the local stores or shops to sell or barter them for essential provisions needed by their families. We also know that women at the turn of the century could often be seen walking home from the local stores or villages, knitting away as they walked; that knitting seems to have been done at all times; and that the pay for the knitting was poor and many knitters were ruthlessly exploited. These small details give some insight into the life of the early knitters. Even today many knitters still work directly for shops, fortunately the conditions are radically changed. The tables have slowly been turning, and good knitters are now much in demand and so have to be well treated. There is much competition between producers for the skilled knitters, and there is a saying 'good knitters must be treated like bone china'. This goes back to the time when bone china was enormously expensive and really prized.

It is interesting to note the absence in the photographic records of any early photographs of the dyeing of yarn, such an important element in the production of brightly coloured pieces of knitting. The art of making natural dyes is known to have been practised in Shetland, with the colours obtained determined by the local plants. However by 1840, madder, indigo and logwood had been imported and were in general use. Between 1900 and World War I many great changes took place, both in the yarn content of the knitting and the dyeing of the

Lerwick Street – showing life around fifty years ago.

C.S

yarns. This was a period when many new chemical dyes were introduced, making colours possible that were unimaginable before. With the introduction of these over the last fifty years, so the demise of the natural dyes has occurred. This is not to be wondered at, when contemplating the work involved in producing vegetable dyes which had to be done alongside all the other jobs that the knitters had to do, as well as run a home and family. Chemical dyes must have come as a great relief and at the same time provided a far greater range of colours.

The following description illustrates what was entailed in making just one, red-coloured natural dye. The lichen from which it was made (*Lecanora tartorea*) was scraped from rocks. Once gathered, it was steeped in stale urine for three weeks and exposed constantly to a gentle heat (imagine the smell). The mixture was then drained of any excess liquid and made into cakes of half to one pound in weight. These were then wrapped up in dock leaves and hung up in peat smoke to dry. The latter was easily provided as all the crofts and cottages had, and many still have, peat fires. From this story it is easy to see how labour-intensive the use of natural dyes was and the really hard work involved in producing them. Fortunately, the flocks of Shetland sheep have always provided fleece in a variety of natural colours to augment the dyed colours. Many shades of these have always been available, which along with clever mixing during the spinning process, can provide a great variety of shades of greys, browns, beiges and blacks.

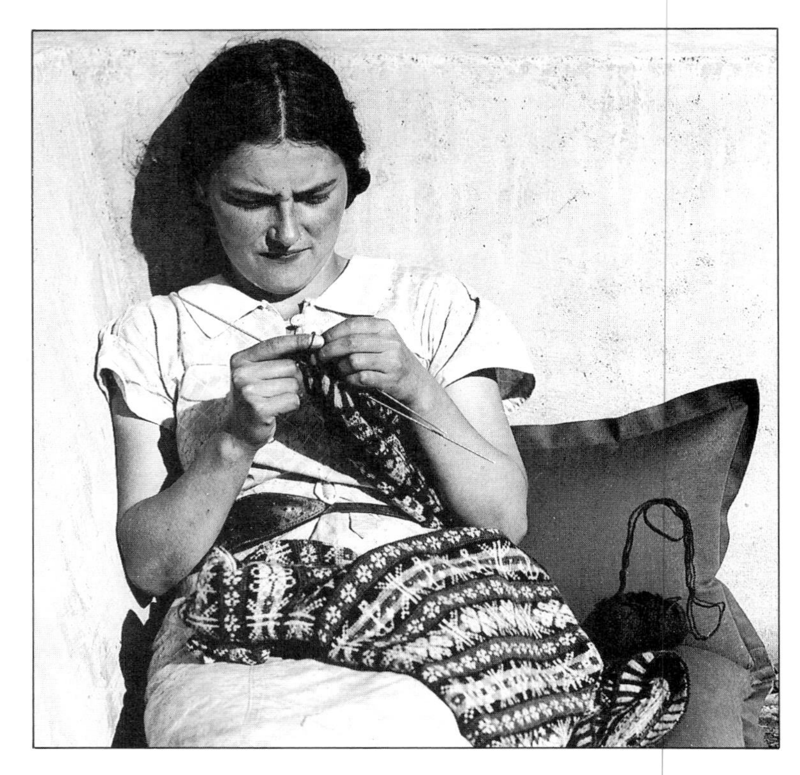

Knitting out of doors in the thirties.

SPINNING A YARN

At first, all the spinning and carding of the fleece was done by hand. Around 1900, the demand for knitwear was such that not enough yarn could be spun by hand on Shetland, so much of the fleece was sent over to Bora in Scotland to be mixed with other fleece and spun into yarn. This was never thought to be satisfactory and the idea of exporting fleece and reimporting yarn to be knitted up and exported again, was deplored by many of the islanders. One island family deeply involved in knitting and spinning is the Jamiesons. Back in 1893, the Jamiesons owned a grocery shop and to this store the knitters brought their goods to sell or barter. Years later, when hand spinning could not accommodate the demand for spun yarn, the second generation of the family became agents for the exporting of Shetland wool to Bora and then the reimporting of the spun yarn. The third generation of Jamieson's were responsible for introducing industrial spinning onto the Shetland Islands. The tale goes that the present Mr Jamieson, senior, was attending a meeting of the Shetland Woollen Industrial Association in Lerwick. Such meetings were only ever called when the industry was in the doldrums, at this time 'Pringles' a Scottish spinner and knitting company had just closed down their spinning unit on the island of Skye. Mr Jamieson voiced the opinion that this should be purchased and brought over to Shetland so that industrial spinning could be introduced onto the island. After the meeting, a member of the Highland and Island Development Board contacted Mr Jamieson and asked if he had been serious in his suggestion. The outcome of this contact was the forming of the Jamieson Spinning Company, run today by Peter Jamieson who is the fourth generation of the family to be involved in spinning and knitting on Shetland. So, after a lapse of around seventy years, spinning in quantity was once again started on Shetland, this time industrially. There is, however, a big difference between the yarn spun by the Jamieson company today and that which had previously been reimported from Bora. All the reimported yarn had been mixed and had never exceeded 60% pure Shetland. From the start, the Jamiesons produced 100% pure Shetland yarn. Since 1978, the company has continued to grow and is now well established, producing wholesale, retail and mail order knitwear, alongside the spinning of yarn. Today, the company boasts a colour card with over one hundred shades and tonal mixtures on it. The mixtures in any company's yarns are important to the island knitters, as it is from these that they achieve many of their most sophisticated colourings and effects.

The early fairisles were often knitted in bright colours and mixtures of yarns. There are examples of sweaters from the 1930s, knitted in combinations of wool and silk and others knitted in lambs' wool. It was not until the Second World War that 100% Shetland sweaters started to be produced. These gained in popularity and by the late 1980s, the majority of sweaters knitted were in 100% Shetland yarn. The trend at the beginning of the 1990s is once again moving to a softer handle, but with the production of super soft Shetland wool, there seems little reason why 100% Shetland wool sweaters should not continue.

The first mechanical machines were introduced onto the islands around 1925 and by 1930 the local companies of J M Adie of Voe, John Tullock and L J Smith had them working. By the 1950s, the knitters themselves had introduced the Japanese hand frame knitting machines into their own homes and so enabled the production of knitwear to increase considerably. The introduction of hand frame machines made the single greatest difference to the knitters.

FINISHING DETAILS

In the beginning, only the body and sleeves of the sweaters were machine knitted, with fairisle yokes knitted on by hand later. But, as the Japanese machine makers produced more sophisticated machines and the knitters became more skilled at using them, so it became possible to produce patterns and then allover fairisle sweaters. Over the last thirty years, the skills of machine knitting have improved dramatically. The designs have become so sophisticated that it is possible to produce garments as desirable as those hand knitted in earlier times.

There are people who would say machine knitting has destroyed much of the real art of fairisle knitting, this is simply not so. Certainly at the beginning, general standards of machine knitting were poor, and beautiful designs were often watered down to accommodate the skills of the machine knitter and the restrictions of the machine. But today, the designs, colouring and finish are of such quality that hand-framed machine garments from Shetland have to be closely examined to determine whether they are made by hand or machine! It is interesting to note that the great pride the old hand knitters had in the finish of the garments has been passed on to the machine knitters. Great efforts are made in the finishing of garments, with details such as the moving of the shoulder seams a little over to the back of the sweater so that the seams become almost totally invisible and effects no distortion on the natural shoulder line incorporated into the design. It is attention to such details that make the fairisle sweater as produced on Shetland so distinctive.

From the 1950s, machine knitting has increased up to the present time, when it accounts for 95 per cent or more, of the whole knitwear production on the islands. Over the last forty years with the discovery of oil and all the advantages this has brought, the pattern of life for the knitters on the Shetlands has not altered as radically as in the rest of Britain. Of course, the knitters have all the modern comforts such as electrical appliances which makes life easier, but the pattern of their lives seems not to have been so disturbed as many of those in similar occupations on the mainland. At the start of the century, as already mentioned, the knitters had to share in the running of the crofts and to assist in many of the husbands' occupations. Many families lived totally off the land and sea. Today, oil-related services employ great numbers of the men, but there are still many who live by fishing and crofting and have more than one occupation, just as they did in the past. The knitters who are wives of such men still assist in much of the work, particularly at lambing time in the late spring. The peat banks which are still worked, are a family chore which is also shared. These are some of the reasons for the tradition among knitters on Shetland of only producing one garment collection a year, instead of the more usual two, produced by companies on the mainland.

The annual knitted collections used to be launched at the Highland Trade Fair in Aviemore on mainland Scotland, but

Home knitting during the forties (it is interesting to note the patterns of the floor coverings and aprons).

with the starting up of the Shetland Knitting Association in 1982, it became of less importance. The Association has financial help from The Shetland Islands Council and represents the interests of the Shetland knitters throughout the islands. It is dedicated to protecting and promoting the unique Shetland knitwear industry. Nancy Heubeck was appointed as organiser and under her diplomatic guidance the Association has grown and extended its influence. The first and most problematic difficulties facing the Association was how to weld together an assortment of different size businesses and individual designer/producers, into a workable group. Over the last few years this has been achieved and the knitters have come to realize the strength of having an Association and working together, enabling them to attract new markets, particularly the Japanese. The comparatively small amounts of oil money which have been made available to the Association have been extremely well used and instrumental in allowing the Association to bringing into the island many consultants to assist and help the knitters with a whole range and variety of problems, from those of sizing, quality control to design and shaping. It is thanks to the Association that many of the knitter/producers on Shetland are more professional now than they have ever been and their knitwear is to be seen at many international trade fairs outside Britain, competing with the best in the world.

To give a real insight into the Shetland designer/producers working today, I have profiled three of them here. I have chosen three companies which are run by designer/producers who come from very different backgrounds and training. These illustrate the individuality of the businesses on Shetland and the very different people who run them.

Margaret Stuart

MARGARET STUART: *SHETLANDS FROM SHETLAND*

Margaret Stuart remembers being dressed as a child in allover fairisle jumpers and one of her most treasured possessions in her collection of old fairisle knitting is an allover fairisle scarf with matching gloves and hat. These were knitted on the island of Fair Isle for her mother, Margaret Stout (a Shetlander by birth) in hand dyed and hand spun yarn in 1910. Later she was to try and have these copied and discovered how difficult it was to match the natural dyed original colours. Even then, Margaret's eye for colour must have been exceptional, as later it proved to be. Between the ages of 16 and 25 Margaret studied on the mainland, eventually finishing her education in the painting school at The Royal College of Art, London, mixing with designers and artists, many of whom later became household names. A turning point in Margaret's career was the event of her brother's marriage to Sally Tuffin, co-director of the famous Foal & Tuffin Company. Sally was always looking for new things to sell in her shop, so when she and Margaret visited Shetland together it was natural to seek out possible buys, but none of the knitting they saw in the shops in Lerwick at that time seemed suitable. The patterns of the fairisle in vogue seemed too influenced by the Scandinavian work and the yoke patterns so fashionable at that time looked old and uninteresting. Even so, Sally knew she wanted to have fairisle in some form in her shop. At this time, Margaret had been out of college for ten years and was teaching, but had already decided to move back to Shetland to live and start a business: here seemed the perfect project to get her started. So began Shetlands from Shetland, Margaret Stuart's company.

Soon after starting the business some twenty years ago, an introduction into the Scottish Merchant's Shop and to Madeline Weston its director, set in motion a business relationship which gave Margaret's products a much-needed London outlet and this has proved to be a successful combination ever since, for all concerned. Right from the start Margaret knew that the secret of the early fairisles was the colour and the well-balanced patterns, and these she deliberately started to revive. This must have been a very brave move, for at that time most of the fairisle being knitted was in patterns of rather large Norwegian Star and Tree designs used only round the yokes or in thin borders just above the welts, the rest of the body being knitted plain. The colourings of these were in soft colours, blues, pinks and beiges. From these small beginnings, Margaret Stuart has built up one of the most respected and successful companies in Shetland today. Against all the odds she has developed a style of putting colour and patterns together which are now instantly recognizable as Margaret Stuart.

KALEIDOSCOPIC COLOUR

Today, there is no doubt that her early interest in old fairisle carries on. Continual research provides new colourways and combinations of patterns and these she develops into intricate kaleidoscopic colour combinations which have become her handwriting. It is this work and her wonderful artistic eye which has led 'Shetlands from Shetland' to success. It is hard now to imagine the dramatic effect Margaret Stuart's knitwear had when first shown, or the immediate reaction of appreciation shown by customers. Madeline Weston, in her book *Traditional Knitting*, recalls how her customers reacted to Margaret Stuart's work, which astonished and delighted them.

Margaret's work has been featured in many books on fairisle and she has appeared in two Japanese films made about fairisle knitting. Her home is a Mecca on Shetland to all tourists interested in craft. The Japanese, especially, appear to be appreciative of this, and join in the great passion Margaret has for it. At her house not only do they see her wonderful knitwear and her collection of old fairisle, but also her son, Ashton's museum, of great interest in its own right. The museum is full of the arts and crafts of a bygone Shetland. Of great interest is the large collection of Woolly Boards.

Margaret Stuart is unusual and unique in many ways, perhaps the most unexpected one is that she is not a knitter herself! Margaret is at pains to tell you this, but what she does not add is that she has a truly wonderful artist's eye, aesthetically attuned over many years and it is this, along with her enthusiasm and a marvellous band of extremely skilled knitters which has led to the success of Shetlands from Shetland. Today, Margaret is busy not only keeping the knitting business moving forward but travelling, promoting and lecturing, and this year sees her playing host on Shetland to the Rowan Knitting Tour. It is this all-embracing overview of the fairisle knitting and its history, which makes Margaret Stuart so fascinating and the company she founded so successful.

Woolly boards in Ashton's museum (a part of Margaret Stuart's home).

HAZEL HUGHSON: *SHETLAND WORKSHOP GALLERY*

Hazel Hughson in her studio

Hazel Hughson went to school in Lerwick were she studied art alongside all the usual academic subjects, intending to leave the island for more education and a career away from Shetland. This was the route many young people took in pre-oil Shetland. At that time, careers for women on the islands were mainly in teaching and nursing. So, Hazel's schooling in Lerwick was followed by a degree course in design at Edinburgh where in her third year she specialized in tapestry weaving.

Hazel learnt to knit when she was five, like most Shetland girls, but it was not till she was researching for her college thesis that she became interested in the fairisle patterns: her thesis subject was the development of woven and knitted crafts in Shetland. Spending time at the local museum and researching old patterns and garments, made Hazel think she would understand the patterning better if she could produce them, so she persuaded her grandmother to teach her to knit fairisle. Through this she became interested in the comparison of colour and pattern used in fairisle and that used in tapestry weaving. In her final work at college Hazel introduced fairisle patterns and symbols into her woven work.

By this time she had met her husband Roy who was a sculptor and together they decided they wanted to return to Shetland to live and made their plans accordingly. Their idea was to start up a gallery in which they could both work, Roy doing his sculpture and Hazel her weaving and tapestry. This was in 1974. It took a whole year to make their plans a reality. During this time Hazel was lucky enough to get a design commission from a local company to knit up fairisle design ideas and to produce these in a number of different colourways. This commission was to prove a useful experience later. The workshop gallery finally opened in 1975, after which it did not take Hazel long to realize that she could not possibly survive on the weaving of rugs and tapestries alone, so she began to look around for things that she might turn her talents to. Remembering her thesis research and how she had enjoyed it, Hazel decided she would like to use her interest in patterns and colours to some effect, so began knitting small pieces of fabric, but had to find some way in which she could use these that would appeal and sell to the public. The first items to be made were bags and purses in different shapes. Then came gloves, followed by hats, scarves and mittens, a complete range of accessories that have proved successful for the Shetland Workshop Gallery ever since. Even today, accessories are a very important part of Hazel's knitted collection, which is produced annually. She remembers at the start of her business always having a great resistance to producing sweaters, so these were never included in her collections.

In 1975, only hand knitting was produced, but in 1976 Hazel purchased her first knitting machine and so the transition from hand knitting to machine began. With the realization that machine knitting was going to become much more important to her business, Hazel took a short part-time course at a local school which enabled her to gain confidence and to learn more about machine knitting. This was the start of a period of development which continued up until 1982, when the Shetland Knitwear Trades Association was started. Hazel was one of the founding members and has been a member ever since. She remembers well the first design seminar organized by the Highlands and Islands Development Board. The effect of being exposed to a barrage of lectures and demonstrations related to design and fashion was an exhilarating experience. She remembers how excited she was at the realization during the seminar that there was a whole world of design outside the traditional knitting that she had been brought up with, and to which she had been resistant to. After the seminar she could not wait to return to her studio, wanting to start work on new ideas from the inspiration that she had gathered. Hazel realized through this new stimulus and questioning that the reason she had been avoiding producing sweaters, was because she did not want to produce traditional Shetland ones. The seminar had shown that she did not have to do this and that she could knit sweaters which could be appealing without being traditional. Within weeks, non-traditional sweaters and jackets were added to the Workshop Gallery's range.

From 1982, the really strong individual style emerged in

Hazel's work. It became more sophisticated and has never stopped developing since. Over the years, hand knitting has become increasingly more expensive to produce and because of this machine knitting has become more important to Hazel's collection. A chance remark by her husband about wanting a simple sweater and how nice it would be to find one that was not complicated and heavily patterned, gave her the idea of producing one of her most successful ranges to date, a tweed collection. This was based on the simple idea of using a bird's eye stitch construction on the machine and feeding in close tone colours. The garments were made from squares and rectangles with drop sleeves, entailing no fashioning. This idea was a runaway success coinciding as it did with the fashion towards looser fitting sweaters. With this highly successful collection, the markets opened up for the company and these have been built and worked on ever since. Hazel, unlike most Shetland knitters, and this might have something to do with being the only one with a design training, produces many swatches before arriving at her final colours. Most Shetland knitters do not do this. Even though Hazel samples in this way she still pulls back many of them if they displease her (pulling back entails undoing the knitting so that the yarn can be reused). This is common practice on Shetland and many knitters keep few disregarded samples because of this method of working. There is no doubt that most Shetland knitters work instinctively in colour and this has been discussed earlier in the book. Hazel does not work instinctively and in fact works enormously hard to achieve the colourways that she eventually ends up with.

A garment from Hazel Hughson's 1990 collection.

When asked about her inspiration and where she gets her colour reference from, Hazel is reluctant to say, but with encouragement she reveals her inspiration, like most designers, comes from research and observation of the media and from magazines and books. She is quite adamant that she is not influenced by the landscape and the environment. This is an interesting comment, because once again it is so different from any of the other Shetland knitters and designers.

SIMPLE SHAPES

Today, the Shetland Workshop Gallery knitted collection is noted for its colour and large range of original accessories. Hazel always keeps her garment shapes simple, allowing the rich colourings and combinations to shine. As with the tweed collection, Hazel has the ability to build a range around a very simple idea and fairisle patterning does not always have paramount importance in the final collection.

The premises for the Shetland Workshop Gallery have always been both working studio and shop, even though rather cramped. However, with the continual success of the knitwear ranges and Roy's business, it has recently been possible to build an extension onto Hazel's and Roy's home, which provides a marvellous large studio and new workshop. The studio faces out over grassland which runs down to a rocky coast and the sea. Windows from floor to ceiling allow marvellous views of this, providing the idyllic situation for any designer to work in.

Hazel's latest collection, and one of her most successful to date, sees her returning to fairisle as the main design source, but there is little relationship to traditional fairisle. The patterns are new and in the colouring of these no use is made of the graded shadings, so often the hall mark of classic fairisle. This collection owes more to Persian and Turkish carpets and their colourings than traditional fairisle.

With each season, Hazel has gained in confidence, developing more sophisticated colourings and unique ideas for her range of accessories. The temptation to introduce complex styling of garments has been resisted and the simple box shapes still act as a marvellous vehicle for her richly coloured designs and patterns. Although one has to believe Hazel when she says she is not influenced by the Shetland landscape and the environment she lives in, there is no doubt her colourings conjure up for the outsider some of the wondrous haunting colourings that only the Shetland's landscape and light, so uniquely affected by the weather, provide.

JEAN HALCROW AND WILMA MALCOLMSON: *SHETLAND DESIGNER*

Jean Halcrow and Wilma Malcolmson were both brought up and educated in Shetland. After leaving school Jean went on to college on the mainland while Wilma found an office job in Lerwick. Both were taught to knit at home and while still teenagers earned pin money by knitting for a local company. Both women got married, had families and as the children gew into teenagers Jean and Wilma found more time to knit. Both agree the arrival of the punch card machine was a turning point in their knitting. It was really mastering these and experimenting with them that made them realize it was possible to knit their own designs. As they experimented and developed ideas, so friends saw them and began asking for sweaters designed by them. As demand increased, Jean and Wilma saw that their skills and energies could be combined to produce an interesting range of knitwear. In 1982, they took the plunge and started their own company, Shetland Designer. The setting up of the business coincided with the forming of the Shetland Knitwear Trades Association and Shetland Designer was among its first members.

The Shetland Knitwear Trades Association, along with Shetland Islands Council, gave them business advice and sponsored them both to attend a design seminar in Beauly, Scotland, run by the Highlands and Islands Development Board. Both knitters agree this acted as a catalyst for them. It opened their eyes to the vast world of design outside Shetland and made them see how much they needed to do if they were ever going to compete in a wider market. They remember vividly how enthusiastic they were at the end of the seminar and the longing to get home and try out new ideas. This enthusiasm for design has never left them and it is this, along with open minds, which has allowed Shetland Designer to find its place in the knitting market today. Jean and Wilma are the first to admit that until they attended the design seminar and began to understand how to use fashion and colour forecasts, they simply produced what they liked without any understanding of co-ordination or collections, and just hoped other people would like the sweaters enough to buy them.

Shetland Designer has come a long way since those days and now is a market-led company producing a range of traditional knitting which is carefully co-ordinated and built into a sophisticated collection with a seasonal look and style. Shapes do not change radically each season, but rather the classic shapes produced are modified to suit the fashion trends in vogue at the time. The fairisle patterns are traditional, but many have been modified to fit machine restrictions. Each season the colours alter in accordance to the fashion colour forecast, but both designers readily agree that they personalize these and they are heavily influenced by the environment and the changes of colour of the landscape around them, which in turn influences the way that they interpret the colours predicted for the season.

The Shetland Designer Company does not specialize just in fairisle which is Wilma's great interest. Jean is an expert in lace and part of the range reflects this. The lace is produced by hand and machine knitting, usually in 2-ply yarn, but when commissioned a finer quality can still be produced. Jean and Wilma are both keen to retain hand knitting in the company's collections, but production is proving more difficult to maintain each session. Knitters can now earn more doing other things. Luckily, there are still hand knitters dedicated to the craft who enable Shetland Designer to still market accessories produced by hand of great beauty and intricacy. The gloves in particular are knitted works of art, with the old patterns covering the whole glove, including the fingers. The designs of these can have altered little over the last decade. Together with the hats, they are wonderful examples of the hand-knitting skills still possessed by knitters in the islands today.

NEW COLLECTIONS

The Shetland Designers outworkers work as individuals, some knitting and making up the garments, while others only knit garment pieces which are then taken to other people to sew and finish. While assisted by electrical washing machines and steam irons these days, the finishing has altered little. It is still a common sight at the Shetland Designer workshop to see sweaters on the famous wooden frames drying to shape against a wall or the house side. Jean and Wilma agree the company is built on team work. They are never too proud to accept a suggestion from a knitter as to how to improve a particular detail or feature on a new style.

Wilma Malcolmson is particularly interested in good co-ordinated colour and colour-matching across the range, seeing this as important to their customers and markets. Since the foundation of the company in 1982, the new ranges have always been launched at the Aviemore Trade Fair in the Highlands of Scotland, but in recent years with a London agent and the introduction of a mail order catalogue, this particular launch is not as crucial as it first was.

It is fascinating to see a newly completed Shetland Designer range and know that this sophisticated collection has been produced by two designer knitters with no design or art training. It says a great deal for the great Shetland tradition of knitting, with its unique pattern structures and colour, and even more about the enthusiasm and innate talents of Wilma Malcolmson and Jean Halcrow. In eight years, the business has gone from knitting for family and friends, to producing a range of beautiful, traditional Shetland fairisle and lace, the designs and quality of which are able to compete on the world market today.

Shetland Designs range of accessories for the 1990 season, as well as a garment from the Shetland Designer collection of 1990.

CHAPTER FOUR

Pattern Dictionary

THE CHARTS AND swatches in this section are designed to act as an inspiration for those knitters in search of pattern ideas, who want to make their own combinations. Most of the designs are accompanied by two-colour knitted swatches so the overall effect of the patterns can be seen more easily. Each pattern can be combined with any other so providing a multitude of ideas.

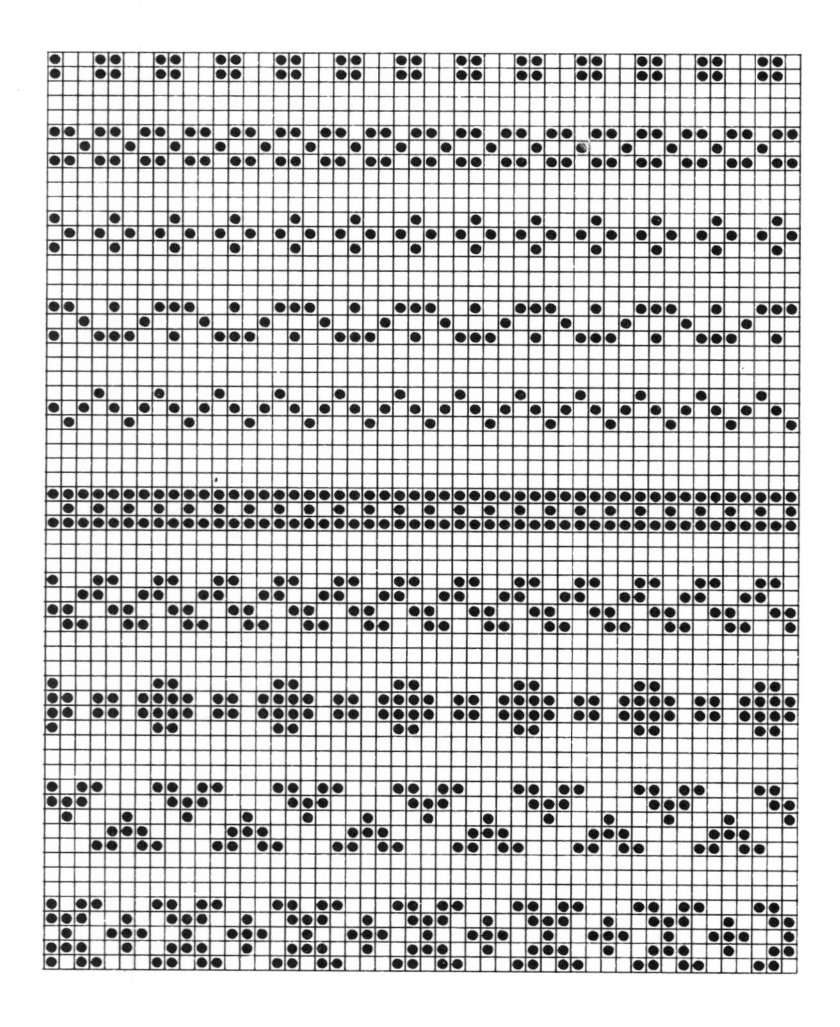

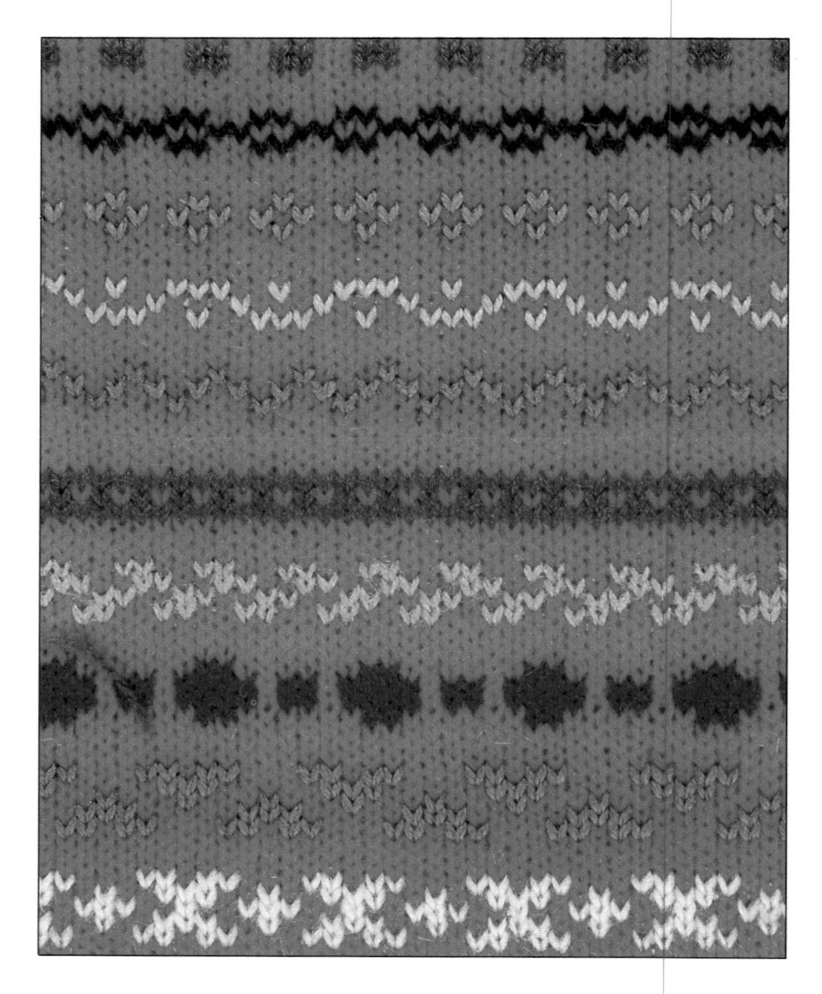

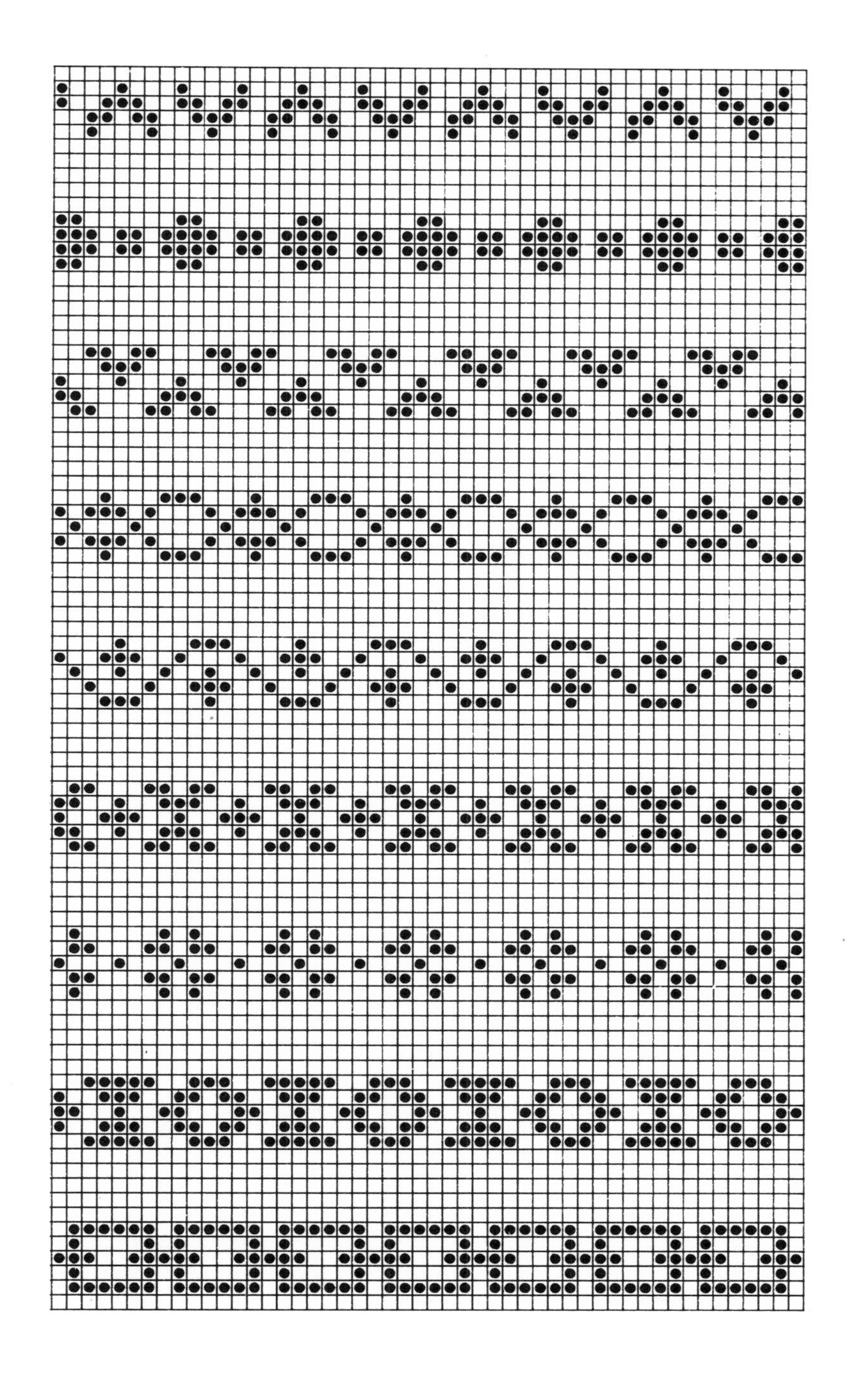

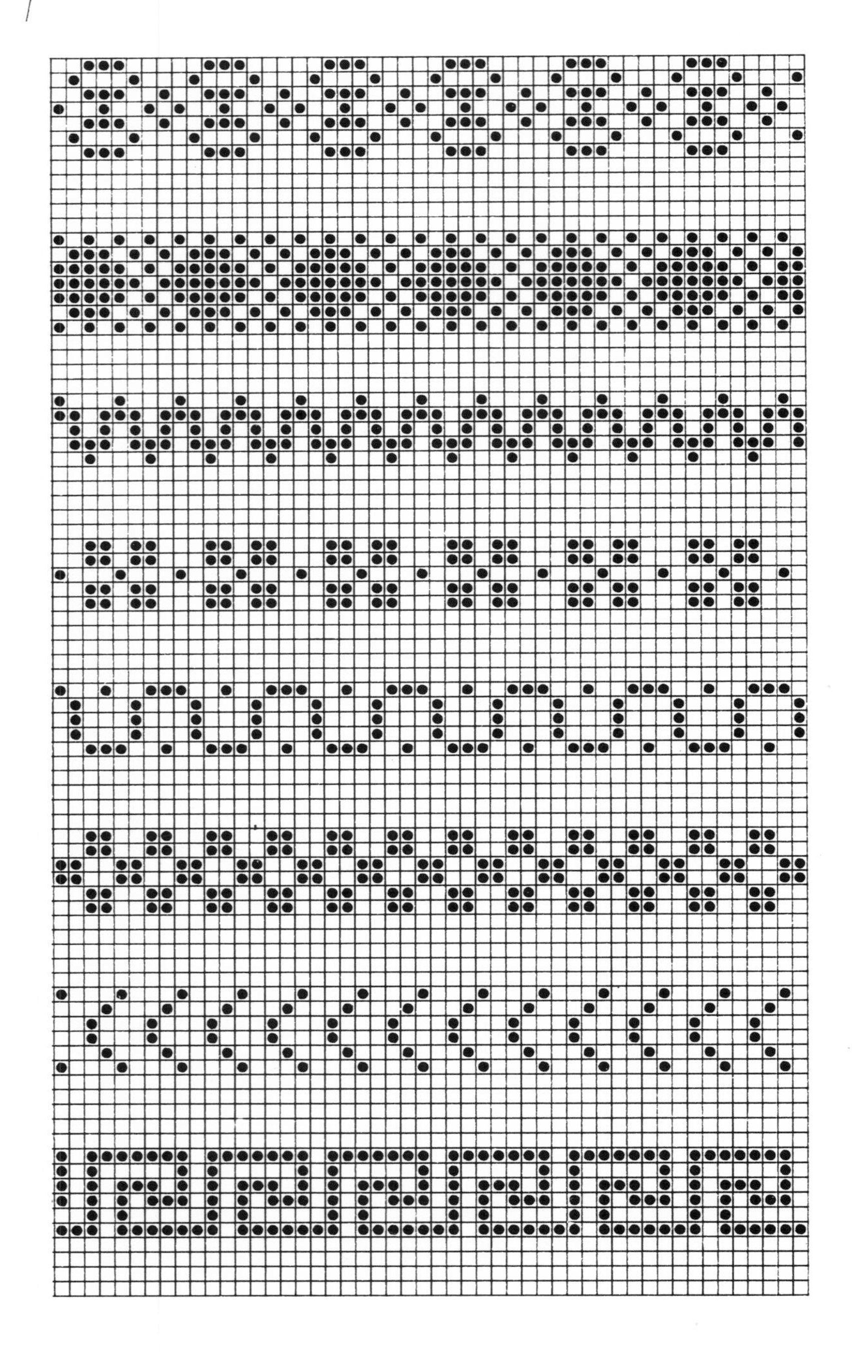

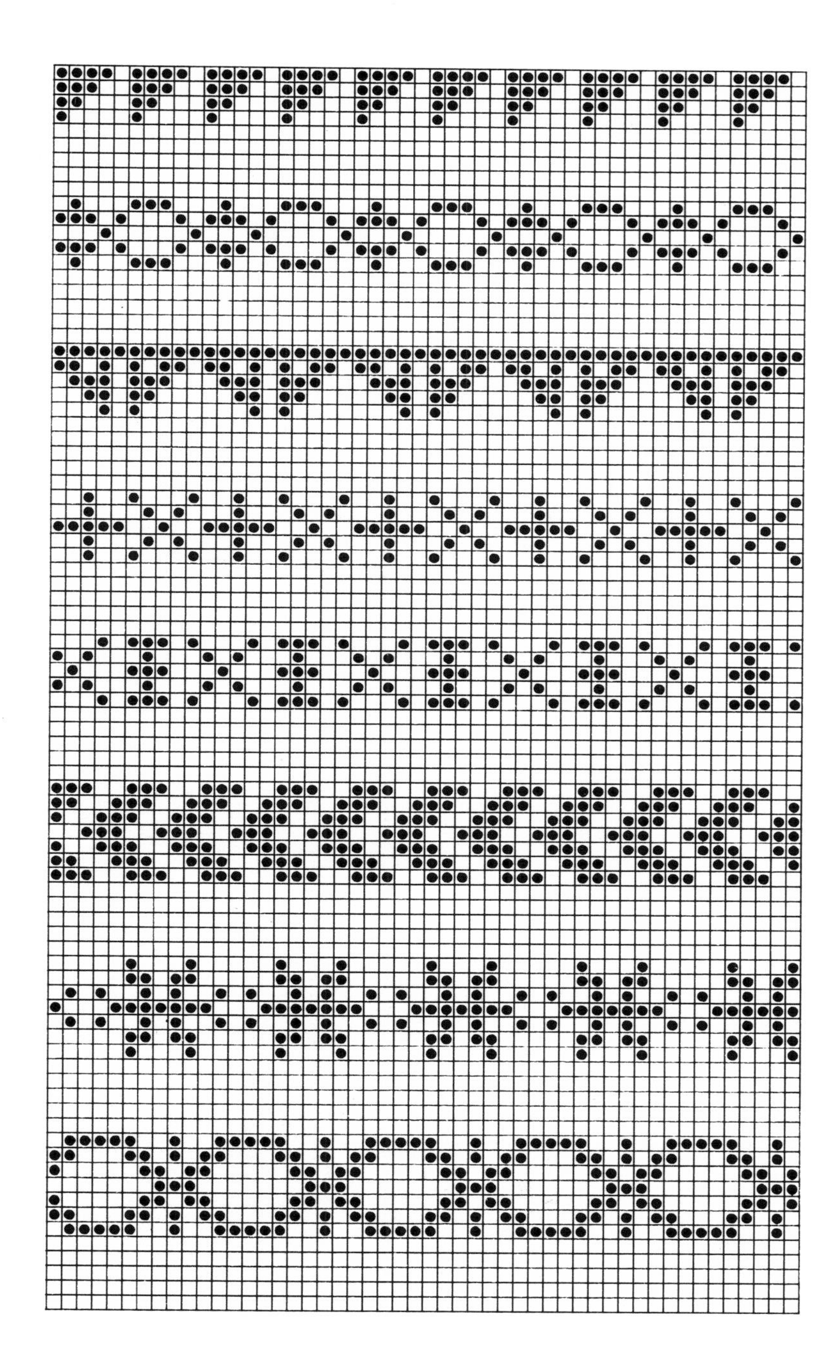

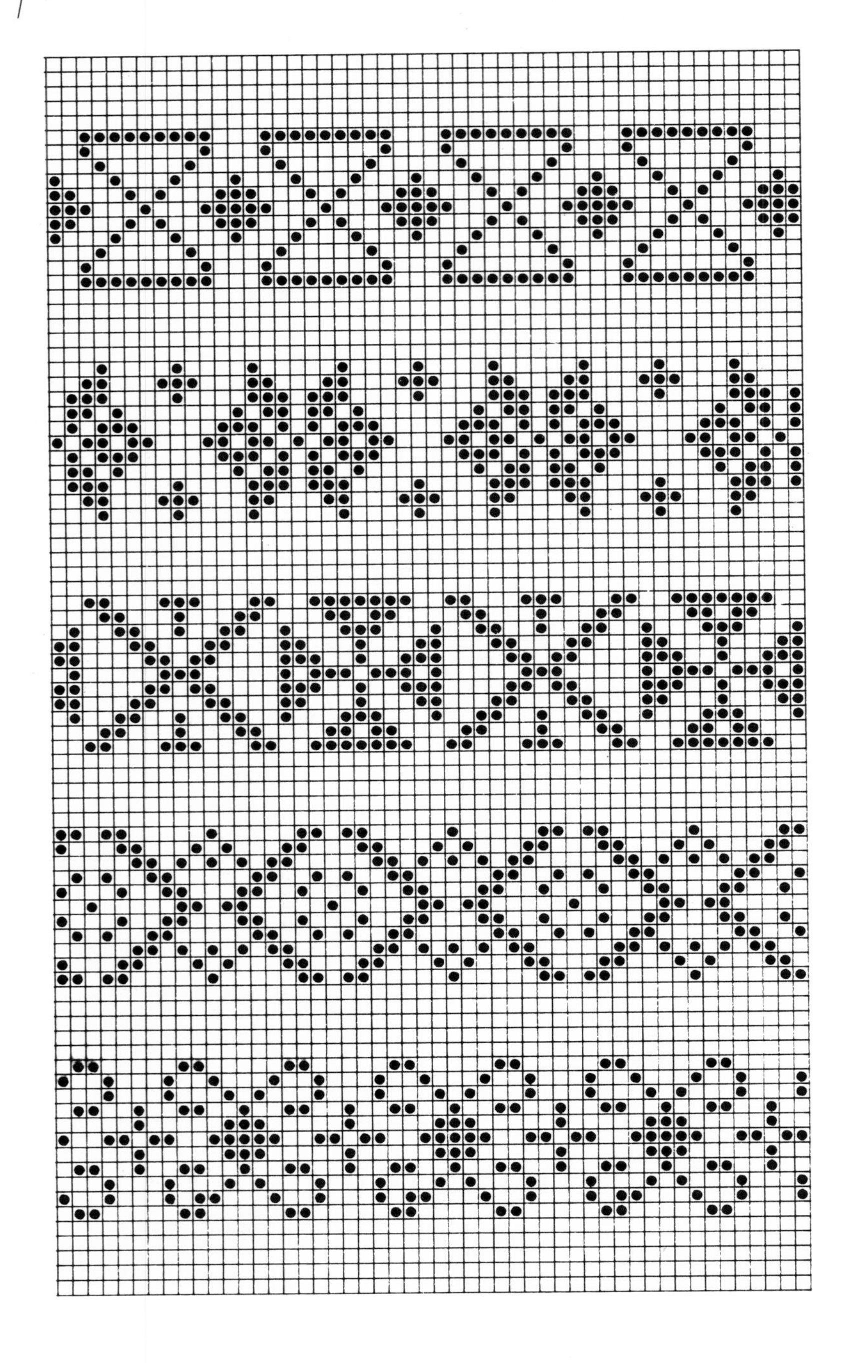

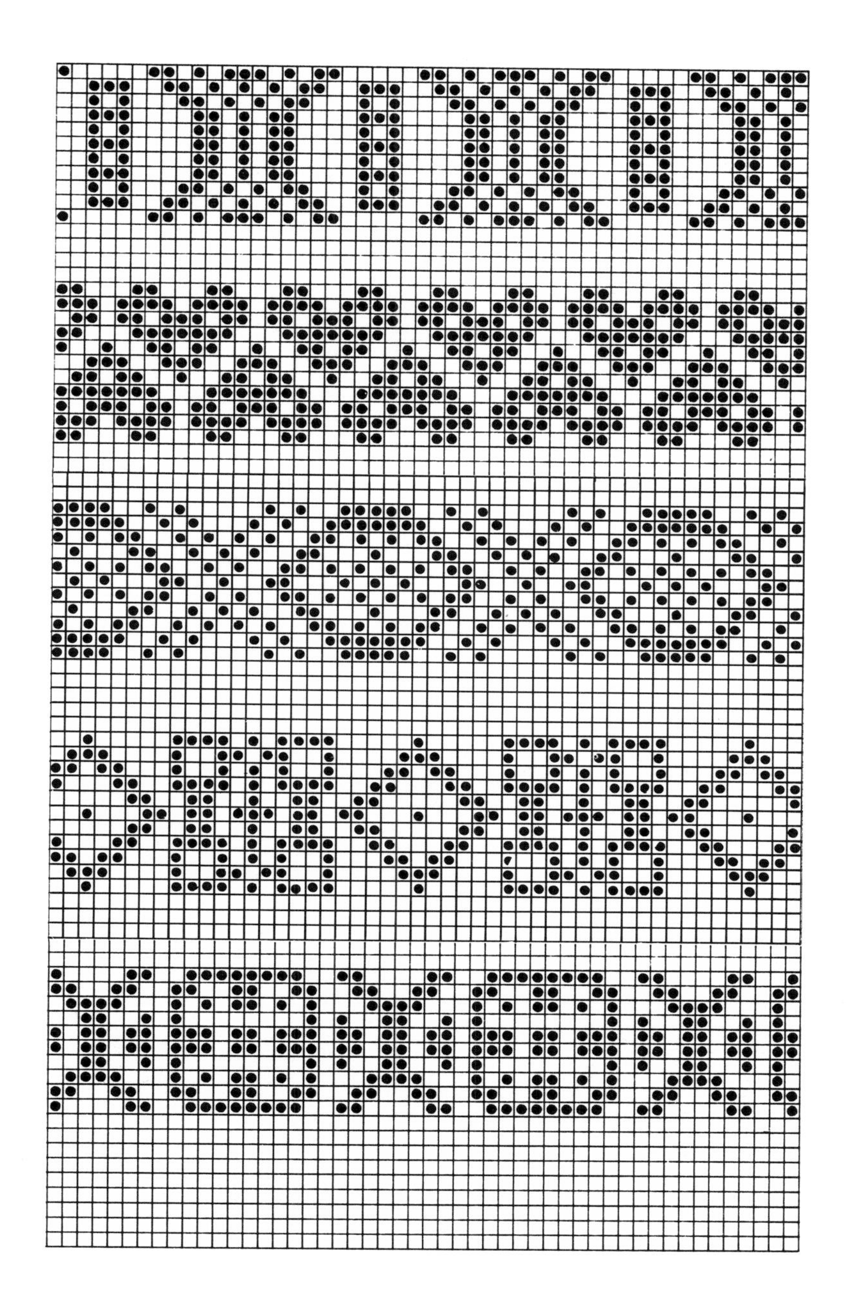

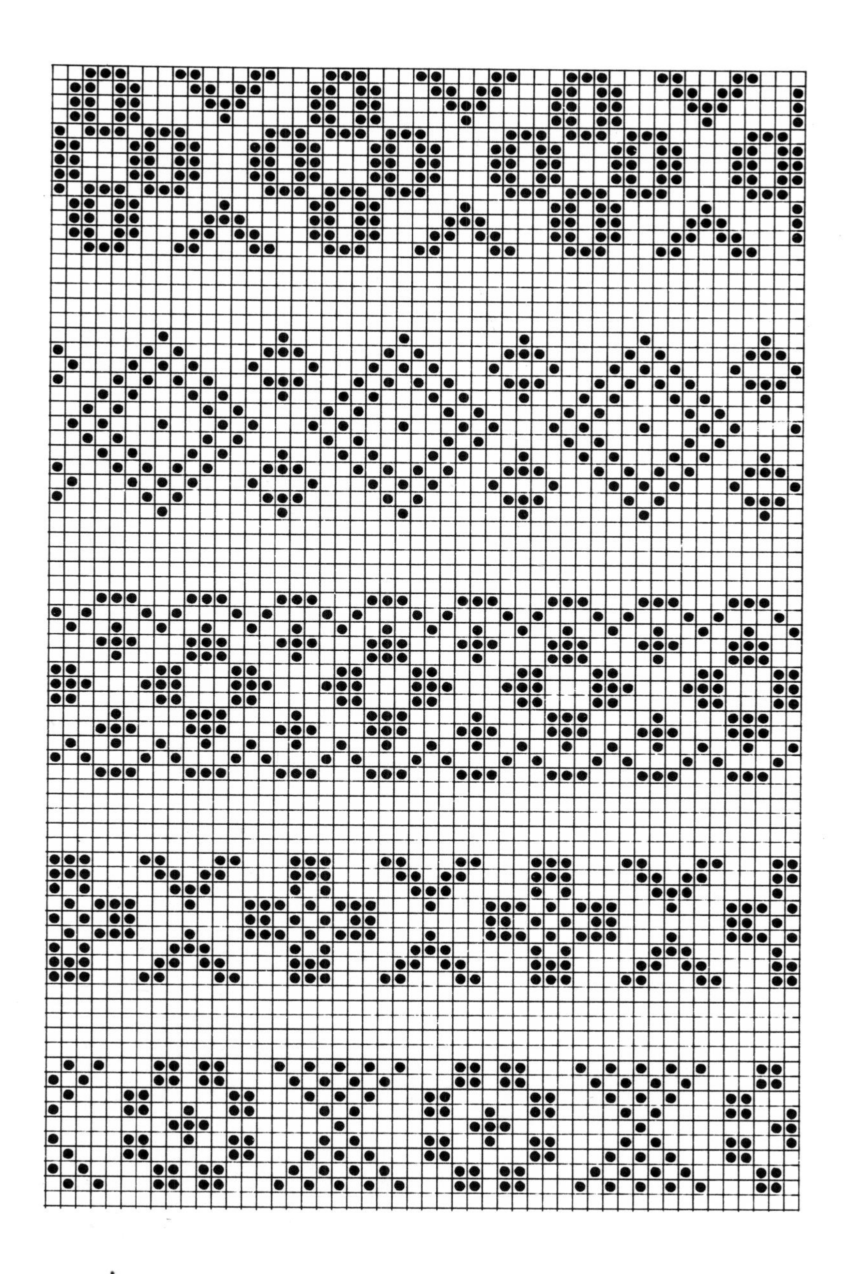

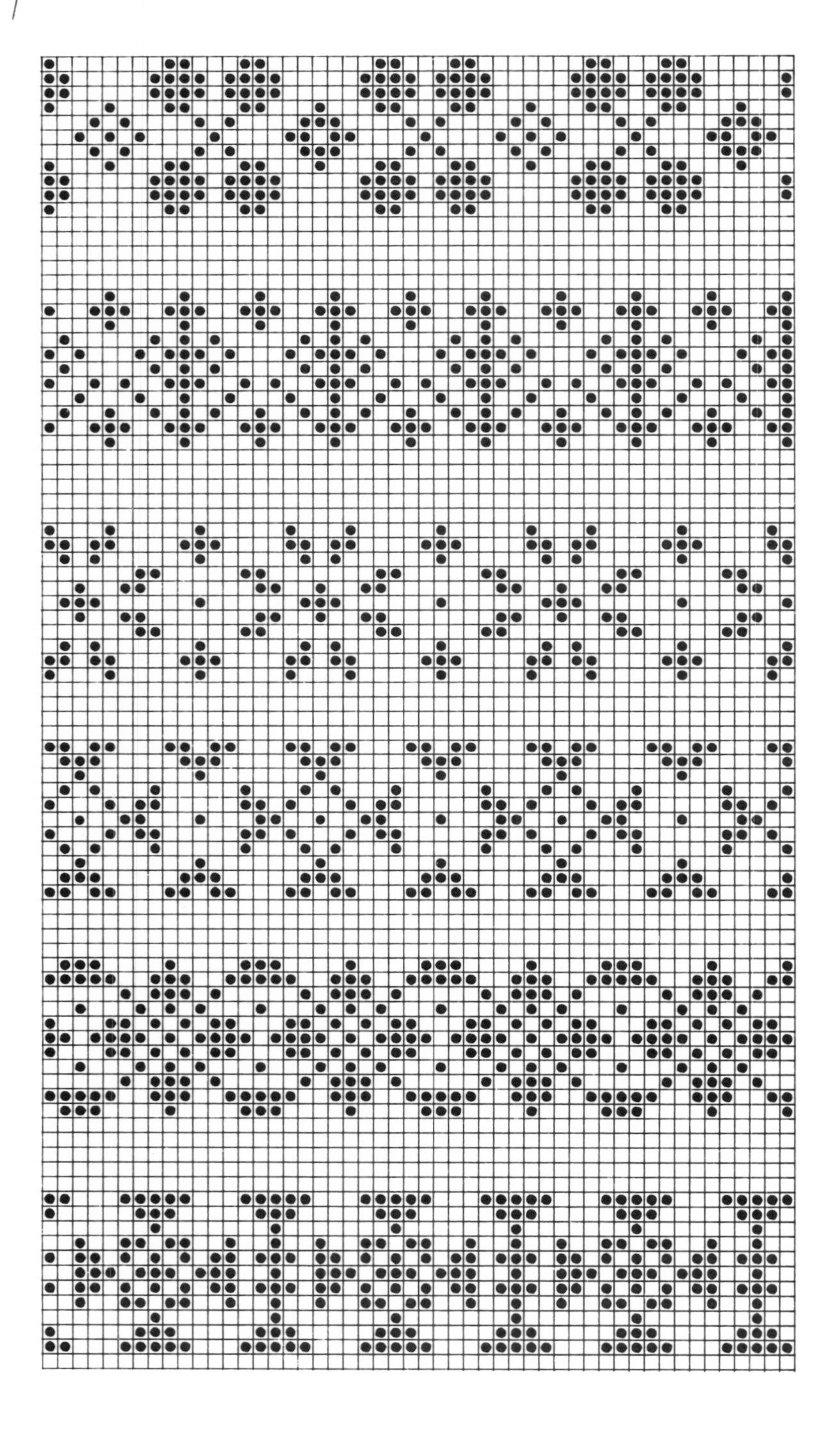

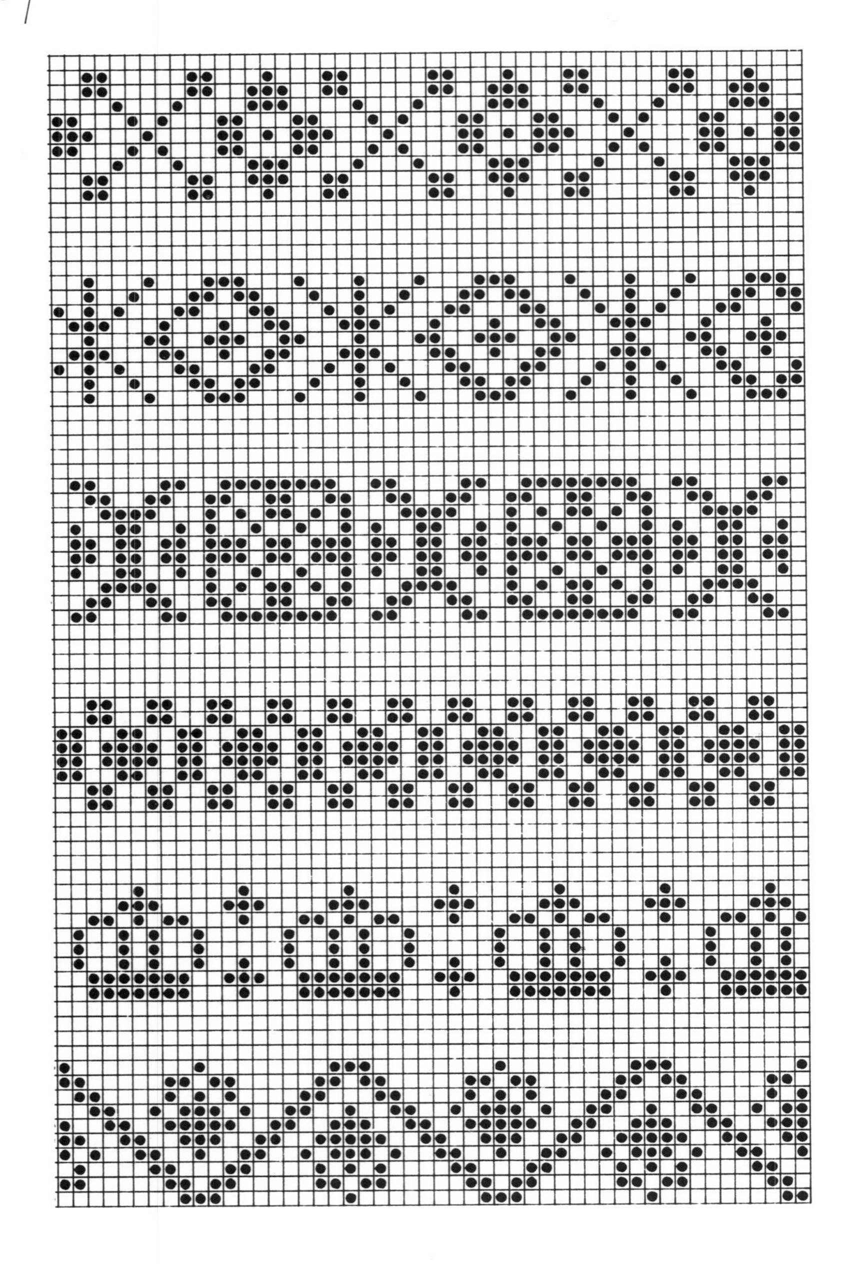

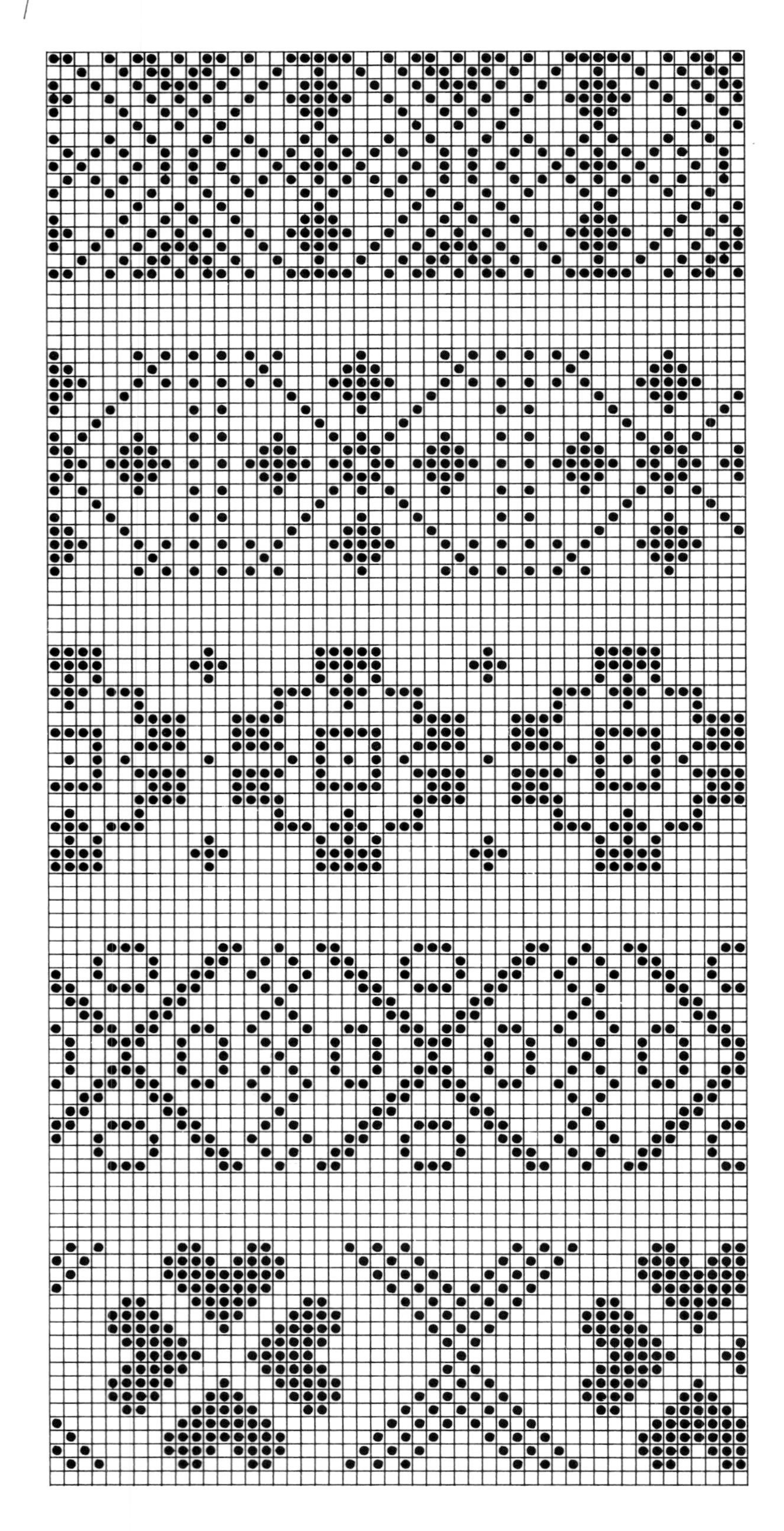

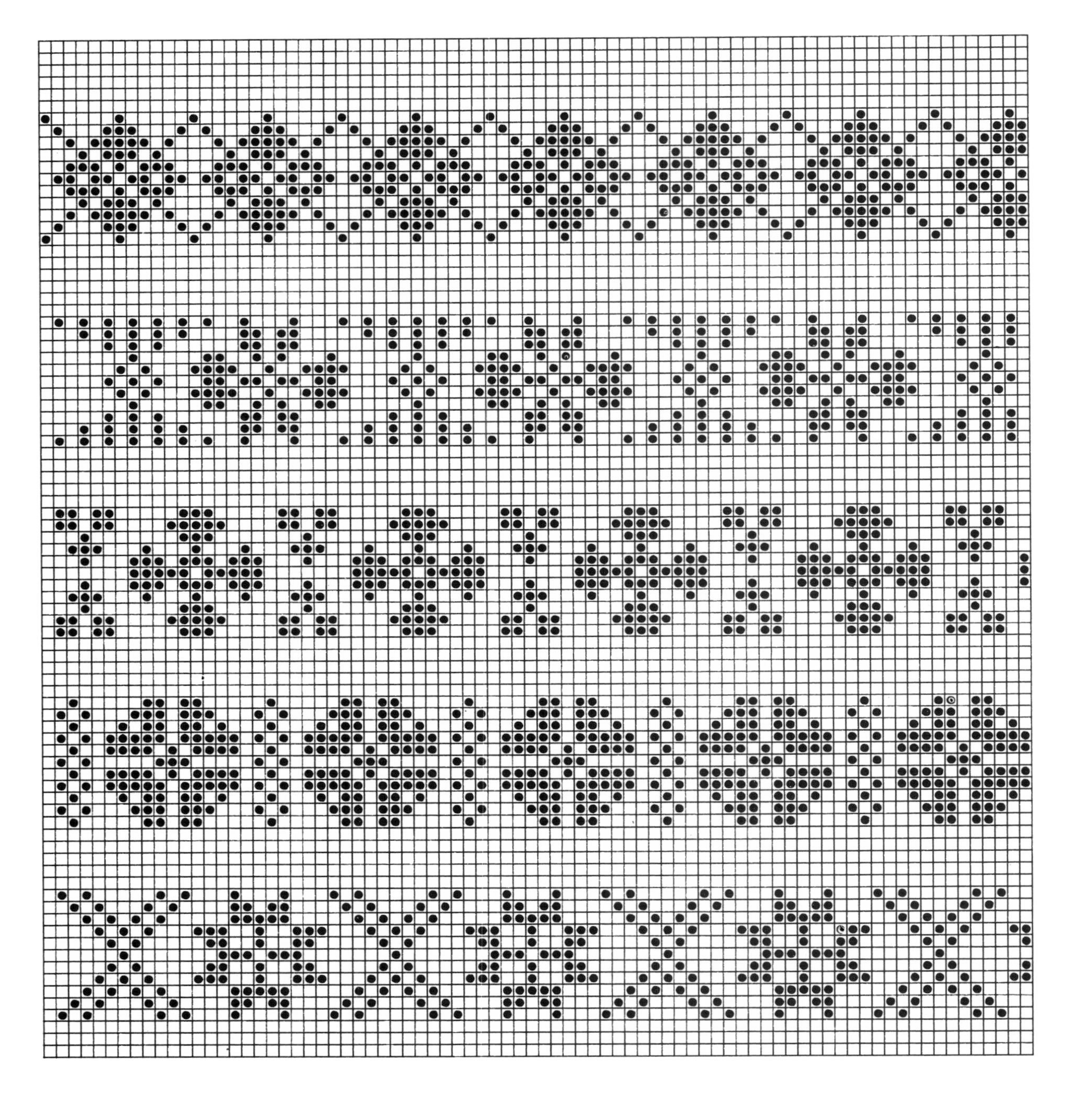

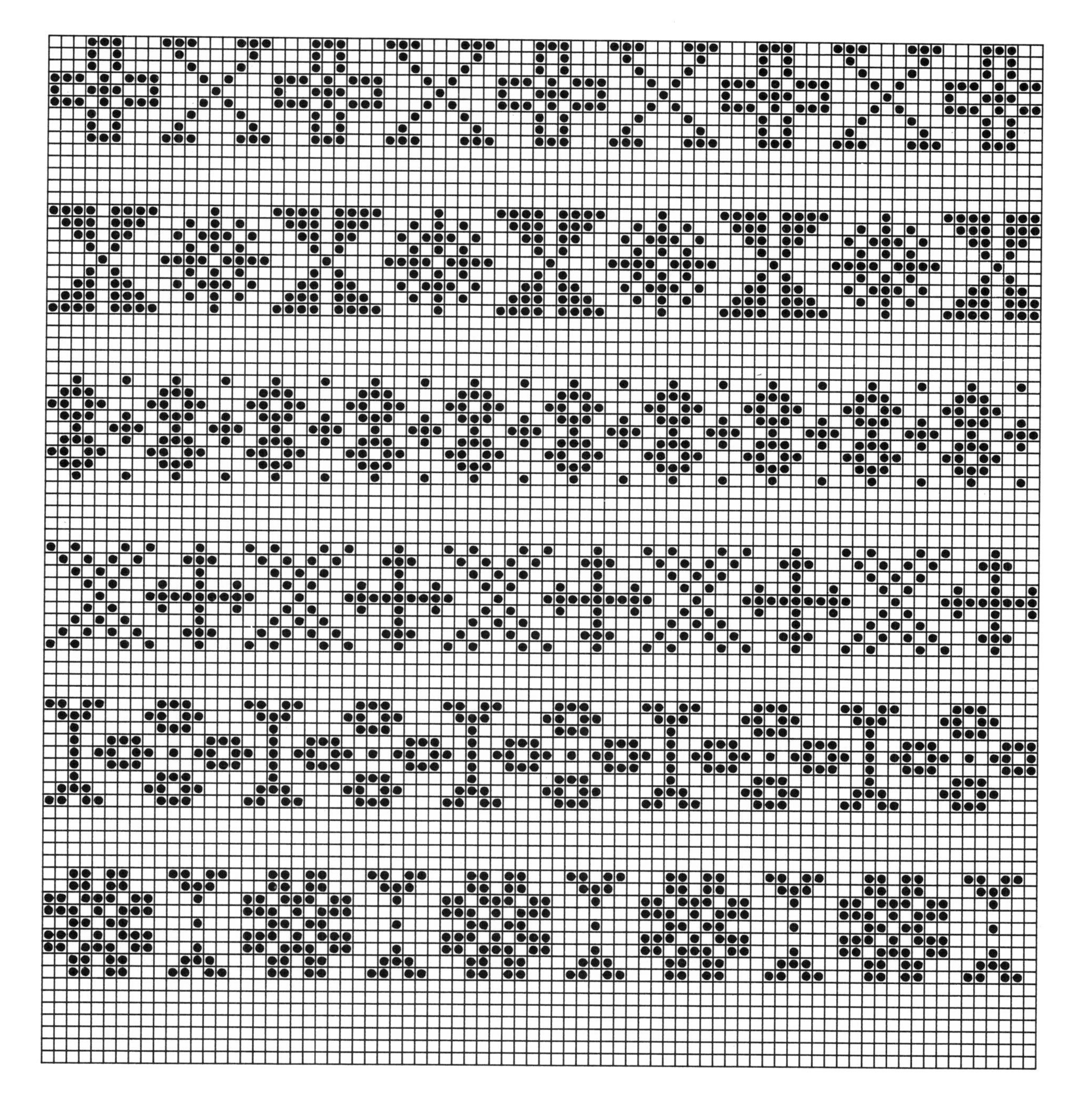

CHAPTER FIVE

Traditional Fairisle Patterns

THE PATTERNS IN this section are traditional fairisle patterns. All have been designed over repeats of 24 stitches, so making them suitable for machine and hand knitting. A variety of colourings have been used, some traditional while others are more unconventional. In this way there is a wide variety of different colourways from which the knitter can choose and be inspired to create their own, original colourings.

Arrangements have been made whereby non-knitter readers can acquire sweaters in any of the patterns illustrated in this section, either in classic crew or vee-neck sweaters. They will be knitted on Shetland by the Shetland Designer Company. The address is provided at the back of the book along with the suppliers of yarns used for all the swatches and garments knitted for and illustrated in this book.

All the graphs which are illustrated are worked in the conventional way. The marked squares indicate the pattern, while the blank squares represent the ground colour. All the graphs are marked out as two-colour patterns except in the case of the garment patterns. This is to make reading them easy and to encourage the knitter to use their own colour combinations only using the illustrations of fairisle patterns as inspiration.

COLOUR COMBINATIONS

Colours can be changed as often as the knitter wishes within a pattern. It is useful, however, before starting, to think carefully how you intend using the colour in your work. The easiest colourways are those where the ground colour is kept constant throughout the work, with only the pattern colour changing. It is best with any design to knit it first in two colours only, such as those examples given in Chapter 4. Then, after careful thought and observation of this, should you venture into more complicated colour combinations. From the initial two-colour swatch it is possible to work out where colour changes will work best, and to plan the colour sequence accurately. Once confidence has been gained, it is easy to graduate onto the more complicated colourings like some of those illustrated on the following pages.

The most difficult problem in knitting complicated colour sequences is to remember when the colour changes are to take place. This is particularly so for machine knitters, where the work is facing away from them. A real help for this problem is to number the rows in your pattern, and at the side of each row signify by an initial the two colours you should be knitting with. This guide can stand in front of your machine to indicate when you need to change colours. Hand knitters do not have any such problem. It is quite easy to see immediately if the colour sequence is incorrect. However, for very complicated colour changes a guide list as suggested for the machine knitters, would be found helpful.

Fairisle at the Golf Club was made fashionable by the then Prince of Wales.

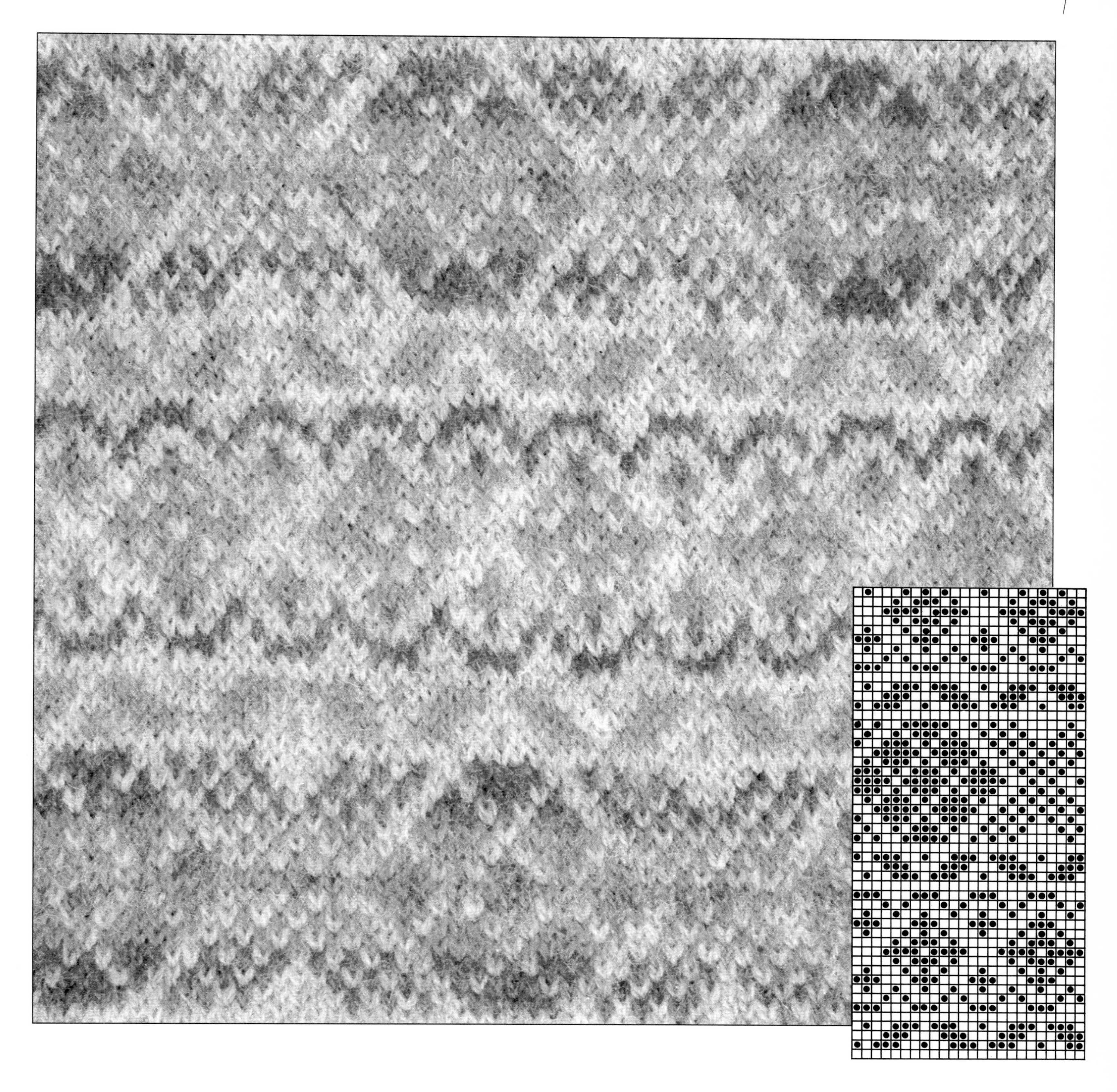

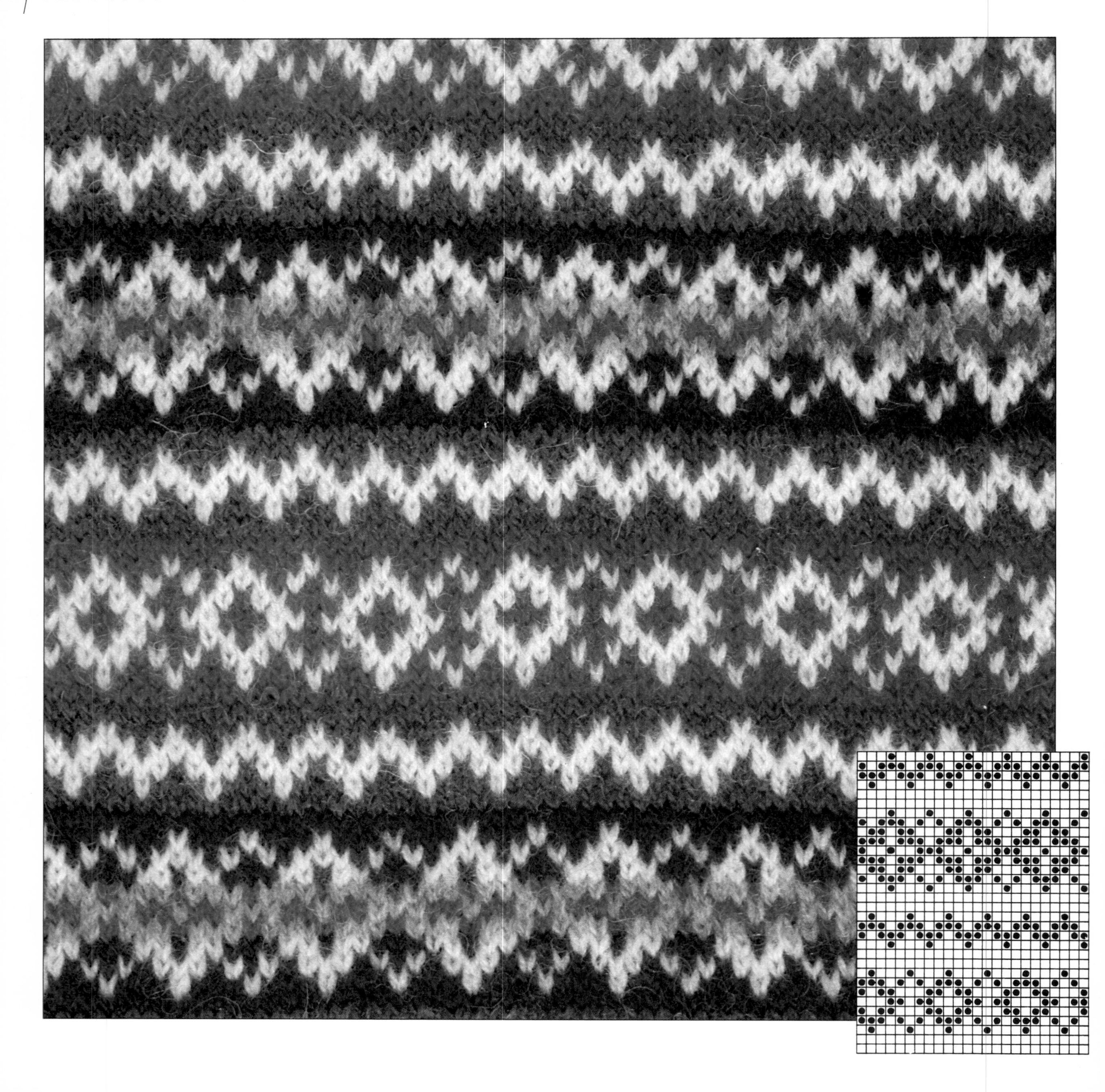

CHAPTER SIX

Chunky-knit Designs

THESE DESIGNS ARE all hand knitted in Lopi Chunky wool yarn. With the new chunky hand flat machines, versions of these could also be machine knitted, but modifications of the pattern would be needed. I have included this group of exclusive hand-knit designs because fairisle is so rarely worked in such thick yarns and I believe these patterns demonstrate what a loss this is. Knitting fairisle in thick chunky yarns means there is a loss of detail, but the gain is in the dramatic scale that one can achieve using such yarns. In this section different designs are illustrated and also ideas for decoration work on top of them. Care must be taken with some of these designs as not all of them have been lined up. While these designs work for hand knitting they will present difficulties for machine interpretation.

BLACK AND WHITE TREE AND STAR DESIGN

This design demonstrates what happens if the patterns selected to use are not compatible, *e.g.* the number of stitches in each pattern does not equate. The patterns will not line up, giving a very unbalanced appearance to the design. The graph shows what can be done to correct this. One complete pattern has been dropped from the sequence of the design, because the number of stitches needed to complete it could not be made to equate with the other two designs. However, the two other sequences of patterns have been made compatible. This has been done by altering the number of stitches separating the star and the linking tree patterns in the sequence. In one horizontal pattern sequence, two stitches are used to separate the tree and star patterns, while in the second horizontal pattern sequence only one stitch is used to separate the tree and star, so allowing both patterns to line up, making them compatible. The small peerie design is not compatible with either of the two star patterns, but as it is so small this can be used and slight modifications made at the seam joins, when the sides of the sweater are finished, but even then only for hand knitting. This can be done by Swiss darning during the sewing up. For machine knitters, it is always advisable to only use totally compatible patterns.

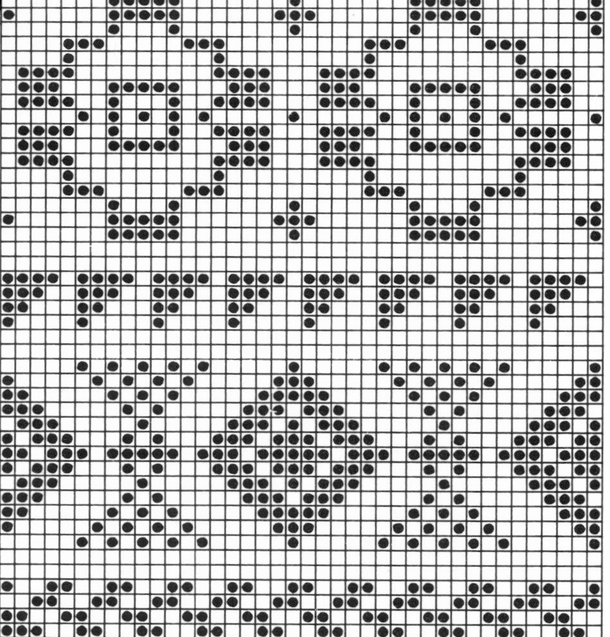

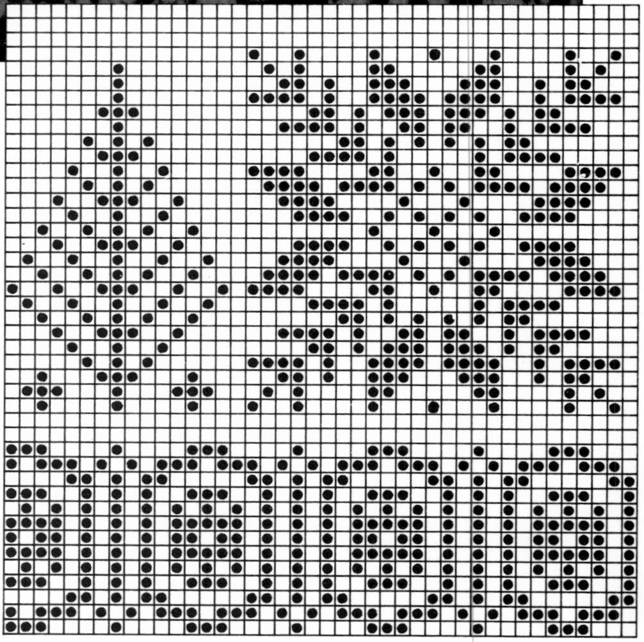

STAR AND TREE DESIGN

This design is knitted in brown and beige wool and all the other colours have been added to the sample after it was finished. To achieve this, coloured yarn was laid on the knitted swatch in the place and shape desired, the whole sample was then passed through a needle punching machine. A needle punching machine is a machine with a bed of needles which go up and down into each other. Fabric is passed through the machine and pierced by the needles. Anything laid on top of a fabric when passing through is punched into the fabric so becoming part of it. This means that knitting going into the machine with yarn on top comes out with the yarn punched into the fabric so becoming an integral part of the patterning and cloth.

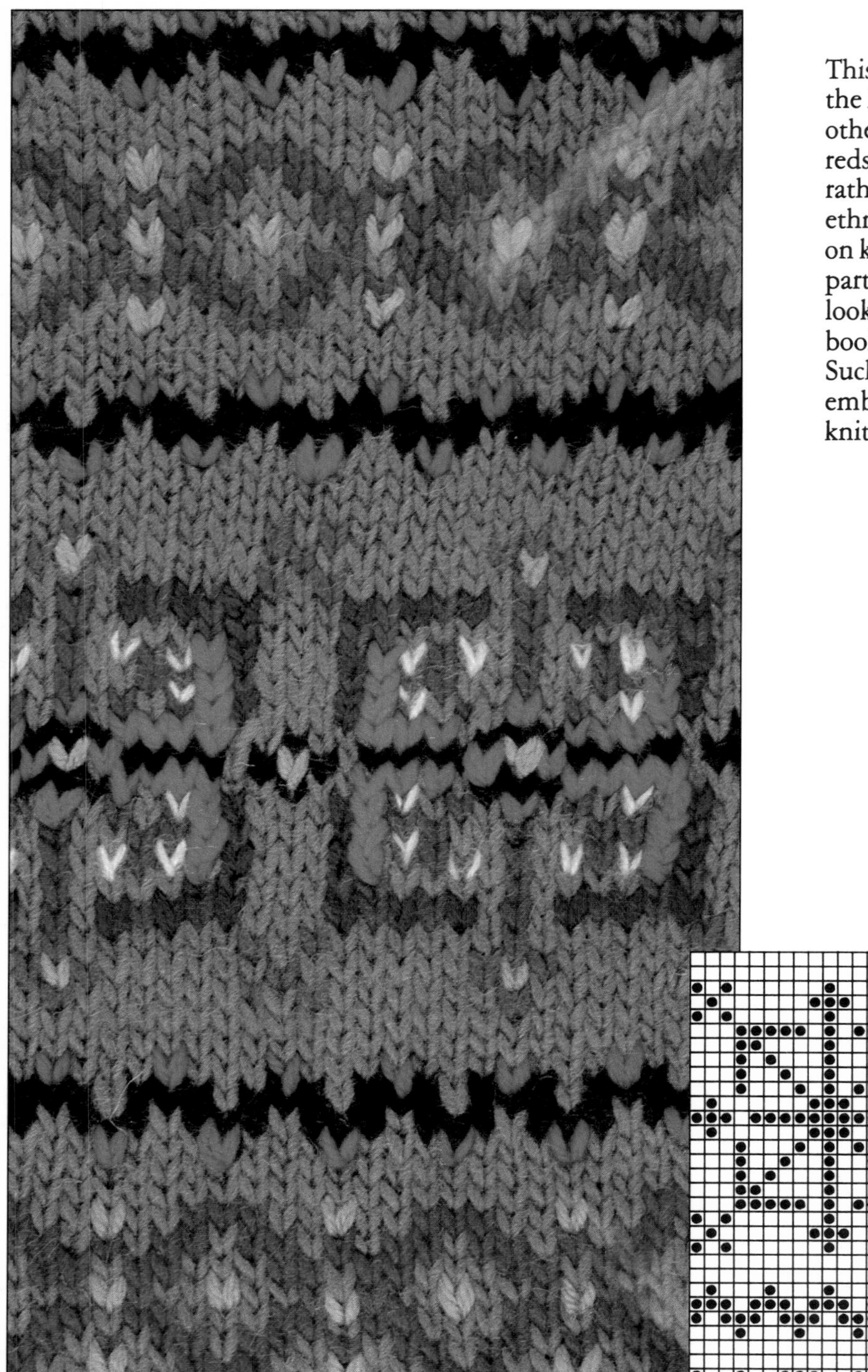

SQUARE AND SHIELD DESIGN

This design has been knitted in tones of greens and blues. When the knitting was complete, Swiss darning was used to add all the other colours to the knitted design, in this case, the purples, reds, yellows and white. By using Swiss darning a very simple, rather ordinary looking design has been given this very rich ethnic embroidered look. This is a technique ideal for decoration on knitting, and can be tried on many other kinds of swatches, particularly if the swatch you have been working on ends up looking slightly dreary, or lacking interest. Any good reference book on embroidery will give instructions on how to Swiss darn. Such a book will also give useful information on other embroidery stitches which might be used to advantage on knitting.

CHAPTER SEVEN

Colourings

THE COLOURING OF fairisle has always been famous and rightly so. 'Patterns that dazzle the eye' is a phrase used which conjures up something of the richness of many of the colourings. Two-strand knitting is the term used to describe the knitting of two colours in a row, when one strand is knitted, the other floats across the back of the knitting behind the stitch. In traditional fairisle knitting, no more than two colours are ever used in any one row. It is, however, possible to change these every row if the knitter wishes, so that although at first this method of colouring appears limited, it is not the case. Used inventively, colourings of great sophistication can be produced using the two-colour strand knitting technique. The way colourings are worked has changed many times over the years, with certain types of colourings being fashionable among the knitters only for limited periods. In modern times, fashion has dictated certain types of colourings, but there are really no set rules. The variety of colourings in this book illustrates this. Some of the combinations are worked in the traditional way, while others are knitted without regard to tradition, the criterion being to produce interesting colourings and effects.

Some knitters do evolve a strong colour handwriting and use colour in very personal ways. Here I have deliberately resisted my own distinctive style of colouring to dominate, but have rather gone for as many different ways of colouring the fairisles as possible, to the extent of introducing in places, other designers' colourings. By doing so I hope to introduce the reader to a wider variety of colourings from which they can choose to work or be influenced.

Try to experiment when knitting colours into a pattern. By doing so, you will find which way suits you and your colour sense best. In traditional fairisle, there are some defined methods of colouring, such as the colour always being changed as the shapes of the pattern change and the shading of colours into patterns. Shading requires a number of tones of one colour which are fed into the ground, while several tones of the second colour are used in colouring the pattern. Usually, the knitter starts with darker tones working into the centre of the pattern with the lighter shades of colour. This method gives a traditional, well-balanced effect. The reverse of such colourings can look unbalanced, but that does not mean it is impossible to make it work. I believe there are no right or wrong ways of colouring. You try anything and if the end results look great, then its right. This might be frowned on by traditional knitters, but if new colourings are to be invented, the knitter must experiment. History demonstrates that nothing remains static, and the traditional colourings of fairisle patterns are no exception to this rule.

In the 1930s, the fairisles were brightly coloured. The most fashionable colours were tones of beige, yellow, tan and brown, but these did not totally dominate. During the War, in the 1940s, a drastic change took place in the colourings. When the service men posted to the Shetlands returned home with their hand-knitted fairisle sweaters, purchased while stationed on the islands, the colourings of these were predominantly worked in combinations of dark browns, greys and natural whites, or browns, beiges and camels. Many people today call these the traditional fairisle colourings. Research at the Lerwick Museum proved this to be highly suspect. Beiges and browns had been used together as dominant colours for many decades, but there was nothing to show that these were the traditional colours or even the most popular. In fact, the colours Margaret Stewart uses today are more likely to be the traditional ones. These have been carefully and historically researched and the traditional colours are actually extremely bright. The word I believe that should be used in relation to the dark browns, greys and whites, or browns, beiges or camels combination of colours, is classic.

NATURAL SHADES

It is interesting to speculate as to how this change in colouring came about and why, in the late 1940s, we see the vogue for classic colouring in fashion. Sometime between the late 1930s and late 1940s a drastic change of colouring obviously came about. This is not to say that no bright colourings were produced during this period, we know they were, but the most popular colourings were the classic combinations. Why and how did this change come about? My theory is that during the War, dyes must have become difficult to get hold of on the Shetlands, so knitters resorted to using the colours provided by the different colourings in the natural fleece of the native sheep. Blacks, dark browns, mid-greys and browns, light greys and beiges, plus a natural white, were all easily obtainable. Add to this a talent for clever mixing during the spinning and you have a wide range of all the classic colours from which to work, and no dyes or dyeing involved. In wartime, this would have been an important point. Knowing the skills of the knitters one can see how this use of the limited palette would be seen as a challenge and from this restriction they actively developed one of the most loved and popular of all fairisle colourings. They also had historical examples of classic colourways in the Lerwick museum to refer to.

In the 1950s, the most popular colourings were soft pinks and blues on white and camel grounds. Usually the sweaters had yoke designs or simple borders rather than allover patterning. It would appear that it was not until the 1970s that we begin to see the return to the rich colourings alongside the classics. It is interesting today in the 1990s to note that alongside the rich, dark colour combinations the classic colourings are very popular again, especially with the new Japanese market.

The machine in many respects although being limited in its patterning capabilities has encouraged the development of new colour combinations and enabled these to be developed quicker than ever before. Many of today's producers change their colourings quite radically every year. This would have been unheard of before the hand flat machines were introduced into the islands. The machine has given the knitter the capacity to knit a colour idea quickly and without too much effort thus encouraging the production of more colour combinations than ever before.

UNIQUE COLOURING

In working out your own colourings for fairisle, some pointers will assist you. Do not start until you have a good selection of different coloured yarns, these are essential to good results. The knitting of intricate fairisle really demands as wide a range of different colours and tones of these, allowing subtle mixing if required. The less colours you have available, the more difficult will be your task. Remember, effective colourways do not have to have complicated colour changes. Some of the most beautiful colourways can be achieved by simplicity.

Many knitters will only work directly from professional designers' colour suggestions, imagining they cannot originate their own colourings. This is simply not true, but good colourings do need a little patience and time lavished on them if they are to work and be successful. Do not expect the colourings you knit to work straightaway, but be prepared to knit a number of swatches, changing and modifying the colours until you achieve a result pleasing to you. Remember, a colouring devized by you will be original, unique and a real achievement. If the thought of knitting a number of swatches is too daunting, work out your colour ideas on graph paper first, using felt pens. I advise felt pens because they give a solid colour and you will achieve a reasonable impression of how the colours will look when knitted. If you have children, get them working with you. Having no inhibitions about colour, children will often provide you with real colour inspiration, or even come up with a successful colourway you can use.

Once you have started creating colourways in swatch form, look carefully at the knitted finished results and devize ways of improving them. When you produce a good colour combination try reversing the same colours; dark where the light colours were, light where the dark colours were, or soft colours where the bright colours were and bright colours where the soft colours were. This will change your patterns and designs dramatically. Illustrated here are some examples of one pattern knitted in different colours, demonstrating how incredibly different a pattern can appear, simply by changing the colours.

The most important element in colouring fairisle patterns is balance; the balance of tones of colour in tune with the balance of the weight of the pattern. By weight of pattern, I refer to the area of knitting covered by the pattern motif on the ground. Normally the weight of the pattern is heaviest in the centre and lightest at the edge. The way the colour works is related to this. Once you have knitted a few swatches and studied the patterns illustrated, you will begin to understand this relationship and once understood, colouring will become much easier. With each design this has to be considered anew. The balance changes depend on how patterns are repeated, it is such subtleties which make fairisle so unusual and interesting to work with.

This may all sound as though you need to be a trained colourist to be able to work out your own colourings. This is not true. There are many obvious sources of inspiration, below is a short list to assist you:

Stonewalls, dead leaves, feathers, fir cones, shingle and beeches, gardens and flowers, sweets and their wrappings and architecture.

The main ingredients to creating interesting colourways is enthusiasm, patience and daring to have a go. Use the many illustrations in this book to help inspire you and if you are timid, simply start by changing just the ground colour of one of the designs shown. The difference will surprise and intrigue you into more such experiments and very quickly you could be producing your own special original colourings.

DESIGN CHANGE BY COLOUR

The designs demonstrate how dramatically the appearance of a design can be changed by the use of colour, and the altering of colour balances. By knitting the lightest or brightest colours in different positions within the same pattern, the importance of different parts of the pattern are radically changed, along with the visual perception we have of the overall design. This re-balancing of a pattern by colour changes is particularly effective when used on fairisle designs.

Note how, in the photographs, it is possible to create a busy design or a calm classic design from the same pattern, by the use of different tones of colour.

One design demonstrating the dramatic effect changes of colour balance can make.

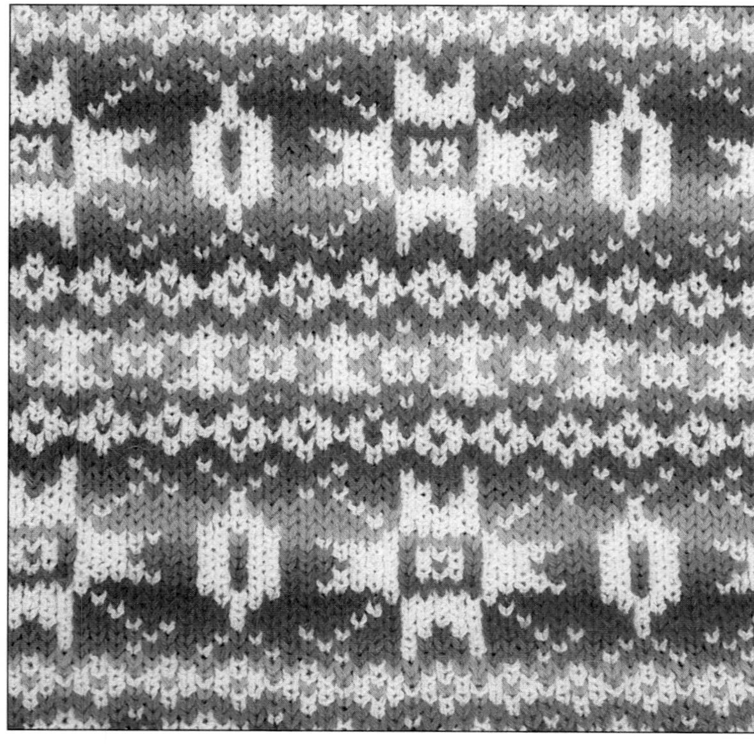

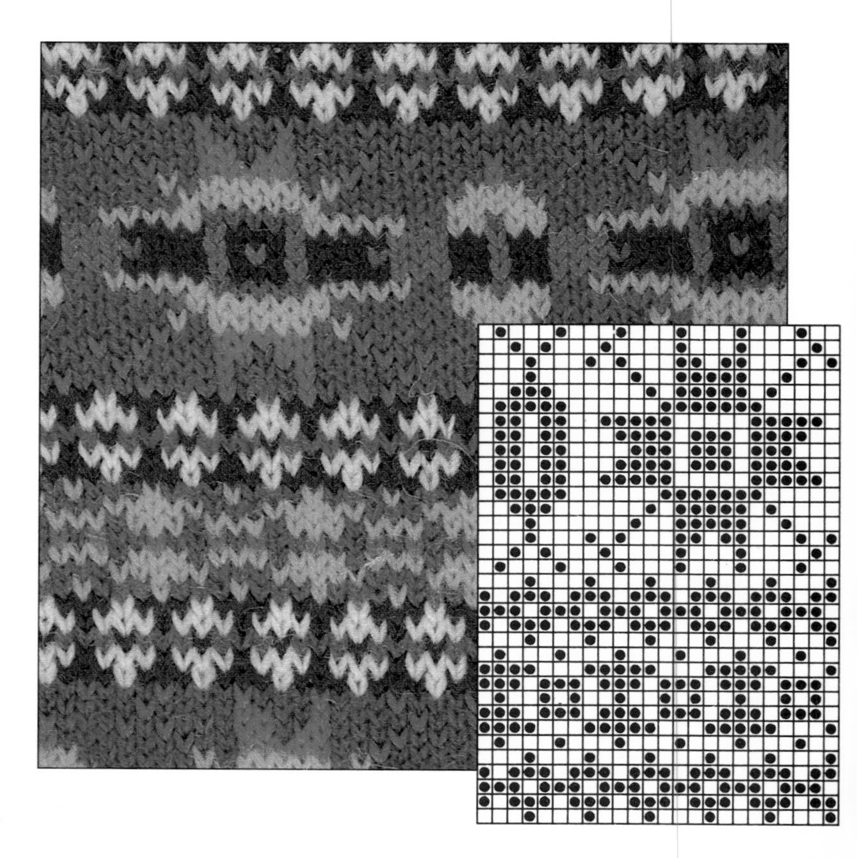

One design demonstrating the dramatic effect changes of colour balance can make.

CHAPTER EIGHT

Inspirational and Unconventional Uses of Fairisle

FAIRISLE PATTERNS CAN be extremely beautiful and there are never ending combinations into which the patterns can be made. In the past, local families developed their own personalized patterns by modifying and inventing around historical designs. These patterns became known as particular families' own and woe betide anyone else who dared use them! This custom is not so strong today, although some knitters regard certain combinations as their own and guard them jealously. One cannot but admire such caring even if at times it provokes minor community discord.

Traditionalists not long ago would have been scandalized if a knitter had distorted or originated new patterning without paying due attention to the historical fairisle ones. However, the introduction of the hand frame machines into the islands made a huge difference to many of the Shetlanders' approach to this thorny issue. The fact that the punch card machines have a limited 24-stitch repeat, made it essential that many of the historical fairisle patterns were modified to fit the machines. The process of these adaptations broke down many of the prejudices and changes are now more acceptable. On the mainland, of course, designers with no knowledge of the traditional designs or ways of using them, have used fairisle ideas in their work without any thought to tradition or custom. This can still be a controversial subject among the Shetland knitters where the historical patterns and sequences are still revered, and rightly so. It is such guardianship, held so passionately, which has kept fairisle knitting alive and has made the knitting on the Shetlands so famous today.

The development of fairisle patterns has never been static. They have continually been altered and modified to suit the vogues in fashion at particular times. These changes have always been slow and, because of this, seen as a natural evolution. Over the last decade, designers around the world have used fairisle motifs in an assortment of patterning and designs. It is interesting to note that little of this knitting has had any effect on the traditional classic knitting from Shetland, or on its popularity; if anything it has enhanced its reputation.

While I admire the traditional use of fairisle and work to keep it strong and alive, as a non-traditional designer I have on occasion used fairisle patterning as a design source or inspiration in exactly the same way as I would use patterning from a Persian carpet or a stained glass window. If a design source is truly great, and I believe Fairisle patterning is, it is not diminished by designers using it in different forms. My point is proved I believe by another great Scottish design source, the work of Charles Rennie Mackintosh. His buildings, furniture, paintings and textile designs have inspired a whole generation of designers throughout the world. At the highest level the work inspired has been original and exciting, not derogatory. At the lowest level, the work has been poor copies. None of this affects or diminishes Mackintosh's work. It is truly great and it is only more popularized by so many other artists and designers using it as an inspirational source.

INNOVATIVE IDEAS

Remember always when deciding where to put the patterning that eventually there will be a shaped body in the garment which distorts it. The placing of patterning therefore needs to bear this in mind if the very best and most flattering results are to be achieved.

Unless otherwise stated, all the swatches are knitted in 4-ply wool yarns. All have sequences of traditional pattern in them, but used in unconventional and innovative ways. The reader will find ideas here which they can adapt and use in their own work. Only a few of the vast number of design possibilities have been shown, but each swatch demonstrates a different approach and creation of an original design.

These designs show fairisle patterns used within large shapes. The fairisle patterns have been drawn into a large motif. When knitted this motif can then be used in a garment as a single idea or used more than once within the garment shape. These swatches are the same design, coloured differently.

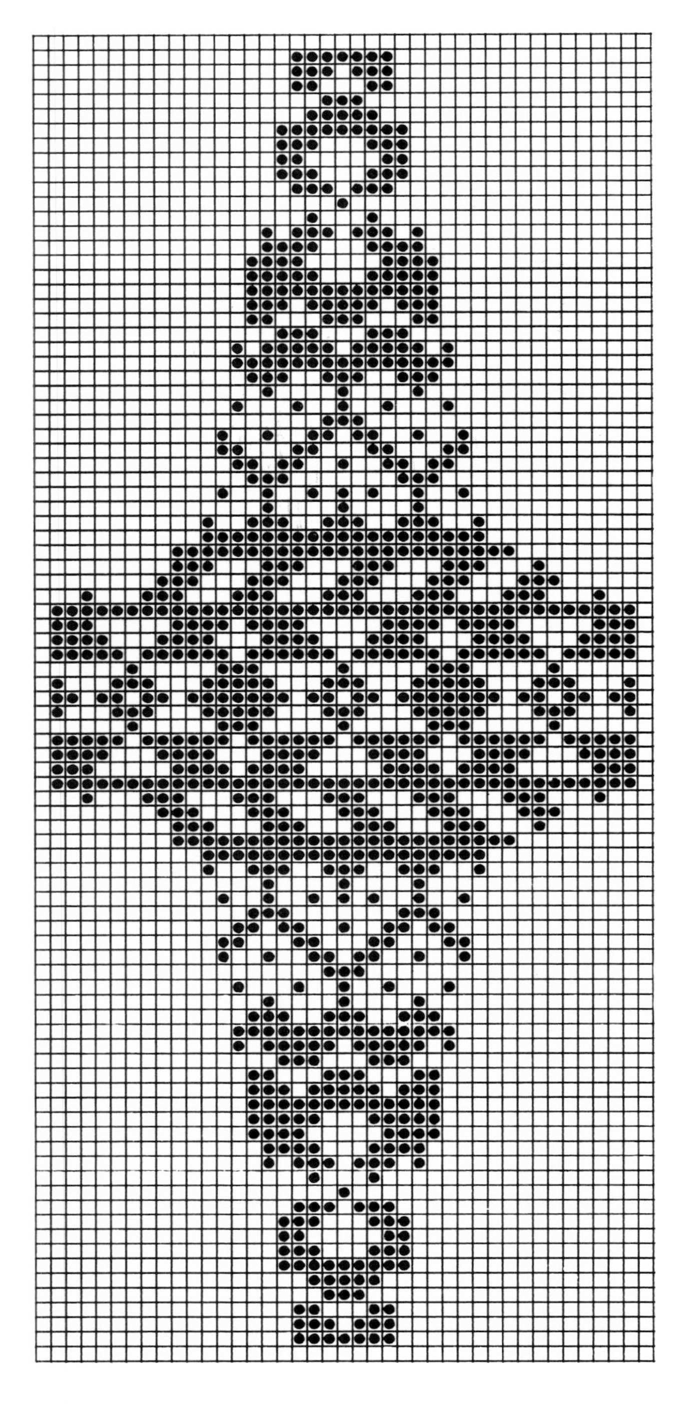

These designs are similar to those on the previous page, but have been knitted in cotton yarns to show a different effect.

The two designs opposite are traditional fairisle patterns using the intarsia method of knitting. In one design yellow cables have been used to break up the horizontal pattern sequences. In the other design white cables are used purely as decoration. Both swatches are knitted in cotton yarn.

Above is a traditional fairisle design, hand knitted using the intarsia method of knitting i.e. separate yarn is used for each motif and there is no carrying or stranding of yarn along the back of the knitting. The swatch is knitted in cotton yarns.

On the right traditional fairisle design using a variety of different colour changes. Many of these are single row changes to get the shaded effect.

Above, a multi-colour diamond repeating fairisle design and above right, a fairisle design with single stitch lace.

The two bottom designs are machine knitted fairisle patterns used with piqué edgings, the edgings give the designs a three dimensional quality. The partial knitting technique is used in one swatch along with the other stitch structures, forming the small pillar effect between the fairisle and the piqué edge sequences – this swatch is knitted in cotton.

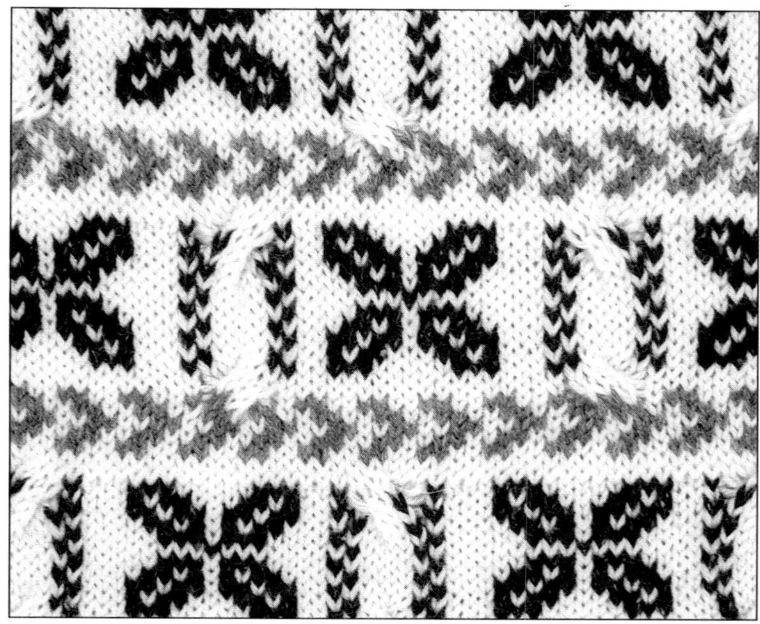

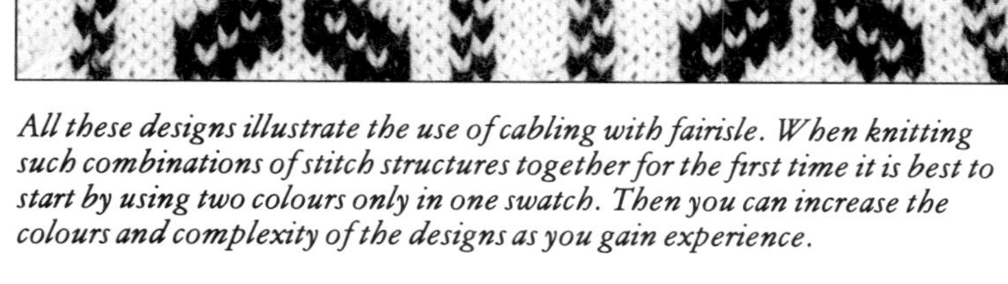

All these designs illustrate the use of cabling with fairisle. When knitting such combinations of stitch structures together for the first time it is best to start by using two colours only in one swatch. Then you can increase the colours and complexity of the designs as you gain experience.

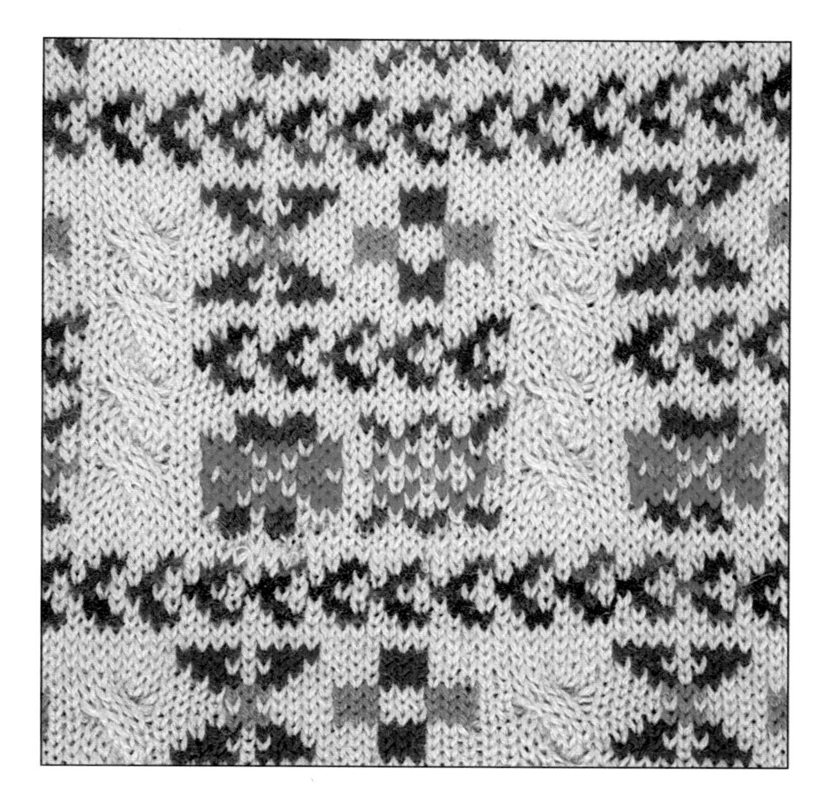

CHAPTER NINE

Sweater Patterns

THERE ARE SIX patterns here, all in classic shapes. Three are for machine knitters and three are written for hand knitters. With a little modification all the fairisle patterns illustrated in Chapter 5 could be used instead of the patterns illustrated here if desired. All that the knitter has to do is to equate the number of rows and stitches in the sequence of patterns in the instructions of the garment selected and adjust these to fit the number of rows and stitches required in the substituted pattern. Obviously, unless you are extremely lucky there will be a discrepancy and an adjustment will need to be made. Adjustments at the side seams are relatively easy to accommodate, at the worst you will have to settle for a slightly less than perfect match to the pattern at the seam. But Swiss darning can do wonders to correct this after sewing up the garment.

The adjustment to the number of rows in the written garment pattern needs a little more thought. A general guide for adjustment is as follows: a small number of rows, either more than given in the instruction or less than indicated, can be lost or gained by adding or subtracting plain rows between pattern sequences. But such an adjustment would be unpredictable. If a large number of rows have to be added or subtracted, it is better to do the adjustment in one area. This can be done by adding or removing one complete repeat or part repeat of the pattern chosen. With a little thought it is easily achieved and quite possible for any knitter to do who is reasonably competent at maths! Such adjustments are well worth trying as success in doing this will open up a vast range of other possibilities to be explored.

Hand Knitting

UNISEX VEE-NECK CLASSICAL SWEATER (HAND KNIT)

SIZES

	small	*medium*	*large*	
To fit bust/chest:	91–97 36–38	102–107 40–42	112–117 44–46	cm ins
Actual bust/chest measurement:	102 40	112 44	122 48	cm ins
Length:	56 22	58.5 23	61 24	cm ins
Sleeve (seam):	42 16½	44 17¼	47 18½	cm ins

MATERIALS

Rowan Yarns Double Knitting Wool (50 grm balls)

Col A	250	250	300 grms	(Camel)
Col B	150	150	200 grms	(Beige)
Col C	100	100	100 grms	(Purple)
Col D	100	100	100 grms	(Brown)
Col E	50	50	50 grms	(Rust)
Col F	50	50	50 grms	(Red)
Col G	50	50	100 grms	(Aubergine)

1 pair each size 3.25 mm (No. 10) and 4 mm (No. 8) knitting needles. Stitch holders.

TENSION

24 sts and 27 rows to 10 cm (4 ins) over patt using 4 mm (No. 8) needles.

ABBREVIATIONS

K – Knit; P – Purl; st(s) – stitch(es); st.st – stocking stitch; alt – alternate;

□ = Col A (Camel)
• = Col B (Beige)
/ = Col C (Purple)
X = Col D (Brown)
● = Col E (Rust)
■ = Col F (Red)
○ = Col G (Aubergine)

beg – beginning; cont – continue; foll – following; inc – increase; dec – decrease; meas – measures; M1 – make one stich by picking up, twisting and knitting bar between stitches; patt – pattern; rem – remaining; rep – repeat; ssk – slip next 2sts knitwise, then K these 2sts together through back of loops; tog – together; tbl – through back of loops; rs – right side; ws – wrong side.

NOTES

Read chart by reading rs rows (odd numbers) from right to left, and ws rows (even numbers) from left to right, and starting and finishing as indicated for sizes and sections.

When carrying yarn over less than 6 sts, do not weave carrying colours into fabric. Place the carrying yarns along the ws of fabric, taking care to leave sufficient length of yarn so as not to pucker the fabric. When carrying over 6 sts or more, catch carrying yarn once in middle of carry.

BACK

With 3.25 mm (No. 10) needles and A, cast on 106 (114, 122) sts.

Row 1 (rs): K2C *P2A, K2C*, rep from * to * to end.

Row 2: P2C, *K2A, P2C* rep from * to * to end.
Rep these 2 rows until rib meas 5(5, 6) cm (2(2, $2\frac{1}{4}$) ins), ending after a rs row.

Next Row (ws): With A, P5(7, 1), *M1, P6(5, 5)* rep from * to * to last 5(7, 1) sts, M1, P to end. (123(135, 147) sts)

Change to 4 mm (No. 8) needles and cont in st.st, starting with a K row.
Work rows 1–54 of chart, starting and finishing where indicated for sizes. Rep these 54 rows until Back meas 55(57.5, 60) cm ($21\frac{1}{2}$($22\frac{1}{2}$, $23\frac{1}{2}$) ins) from beg, ending after a ws row.

Shape Neck

Keeping patt correct, divide for neck opening thus:
Next Row (rs): Patt 44(49, 54) sts, TURN.
** Cont on these sts only and dec one st at neck edge on next 2 rows.
Work one row straight. Cast off rem 42(47, 52) sts.
Slip 35(37, 39) sts centre back on to st-holder for back neck.
Rejoin yarn at neck edge of rem 44(49, 54)sts, and work one row straight. Complete as for first side of neck from ** to end.

FRONT

Work as given for back until Front meas 36(37.5, 39) cm (14($14\frac{3}{4}$, $15\frac{1}{2}$ ins) from beg, ending after a ws row.

Shape Neck

Keeping patt correct, divide for neck opening thus:
Next Row (rs): Patt 61(67, 73) sts, TURN.
*** Cont on these sts only and dec one st at neck edge on next row and foll 10 alt rows, then dec one st at neck edge on every foll 3rd row until 42(47, 52) sts rem. Cont straight until Front meas same as Back to shoulder, ending on same patt row. Cast off.
Slip st centre front on to st-holder.
Rejoin yarn at neck edge of rem 61(67, 73) sts, and work one row straight.
Complete as for first side of neck from *** to end.

SLEEVES

With 3.25 mm (No. 10) needles and A, cast on 46(50, 54) sts and work 5(5, 6) cm (2(2, $2\frac{1}{4}$) ins) of two-colour K2, P2 rib as given for Back, ending after a rs row.

Next row (ws): With A, P3(5, 6), *M1, P5(5, 7)* rep from * to * to last 3(5, 6) sts, M1, P3(5, 6). (55(59, 61) sts)

Change to 4 mm (No. 8) needles and cont in st.st, starting with a K row.
Work from row 1 of chart, starting and finishing where indicated for sizes, and at the same time inc one st at each end of 7th row and every foll 4th row until there are 97 (101, 107) sts, working extra sts into patt.
Cont straight until sleeve meas 42(44, 47) cm ($16\frac{1}{2}$($17\frac{1}{4}$, $18\frac{1}{2}$) ins) from beg, ending after a ws row. Cast off loosely.

NECKBAND

Sew right shoulder seam.
With 3.25 mm (No. 10) needles and A, and with rs facing, pick up and K59(61, 64) sts evenly down left front neck shaping, K1 centre front from st-holder, pick up and K59(61, 64) sts evenly up right front neck shaping, 3 sts down right back neck shaping, K35(37, 39) sts from st-holder centre back, and pick up and K3 sts up left back neck shaping. (160(166, 174) sts)

Row 1 (ws): P1A, P1(1, 2)C, (K2A, P2C) 24(25, 26) times, P2 tog. A, P1A (centre front), P2 tog.tbl.A, (P2C, K2A) 14(14, 15) times, P0(2, 1)C, P1A. (158(164, 172) sts)

Row 2: K1A, K0(0, 1)C, P2(0, 2)A, (K2C, P2A) 13(14, 14) times, K1C, sskA, K1A (centre front), K2 tog.A, K1C, (P2A, K2C) 23(24, 26) times, P2(2, 0) A, K1(1, 0)C, K1A. (156(162, 170) sts)

Row 3: P1A, P1(1, 0)C, K2(2, 0) A, (P2C, K2A) 23(24, 26) times, P2 tog.A, P1A (centre front), P2 tog.tbl.A, (K2A, P2C) 13(14, 1 4) times, K2(0, 2) A, P0(0, 1C), P1A. (154(160, 168) sts)

Work 4 more rows rib as set, dec one st at either side of st centre front with A every row. (146(152, 160) sts)
With A, cast off ribwise, dec one st at each side of st centre front in cast-off row as before.

TO MAKE UP

Weave in all loose ends. Sew left shoulder and neckback seam. Beg and ending 20(21, 22) cm ($7\frac{3}{4}$($8\frac{1}{4}$, $8\frac{3}{4}$) ins) down side edges from shoulder seams, sew sleeves to sides. Sew side and sleeve seams.

LADIES' CLASSICAL CREW NECK WITH OPTIONAL COLLAR (HAND KNIT)

SIZES

	small	*medium*	*large*
Actual bust measurement:	98 38	105 41	112 cm 44 ins
Length:	56 22	57 22½	60 cm 23½ ins
Sleeve (seam):	41 16	41 16	42.5 cm 16¾ ins

MATERIALS

Pamela Wise 4-ply Wool (50 grm balls)

Col A	100	150	150 grms	(Pale Blue)
Col B	200	200	250 grms	(White)
Col C	50	50	50 grms	(Green)
Col D	100	100	100 grms	(Pink)
Col E	50	50	50 grms	(Yellow)
Col F	50	50	50 grms	(Peach)
Col G	50	50	50 grms	(Turquoise)

1 pair each size 2.75 mm (No. 12) and 3.25 mm (No. 10) knitting needles.
Stitch holders.

TENSION

30 sts and 33 rows to 10 cm (4 ins) over patt using 3.25 mm (No. 10) needles.

ABBREVIATIONS

K – Knit; P – Purl; st(s) – stitch(es); st.st – stocking stitch; alt – alternate; beg – beginning; cont – continue; foll – following; inc – increase; dec – decrease; meas – measures; M1 – make one stich by picking up, twisting and knitting bar between stitches; patt – pattern; rem – remaining; rep – repeat; tog – together; rs – right side; ws – wrong side.

NOTES

Read chart by reading rs rows (odd numbers) from right to left, and ws rows (even numbers) from left to right, and starting and finishing as indicated for sizes and sections.

When carrying yarn over less than 6 sts, do not weave carrying colours into fabric. Place the carrying yarns along the ws of fabric, taking care to leave sufficient length of yarn so as not to pucker the fabric. When carrying over 6 sts or more, catch carrying yarn once in middle of carry.

To match patt underarm, sleeve patt starts on rows 45(49, 49) of body chart. Should longer or shorter sleeves be required, adjust length by starting patt on appropriate row.

BACK

With 2.75 mm (No. 12) needles and A, cast on 134(146, 154) sts.
Row 1 (rs): K2, *P2, K2* rep from * to * to end.
Row 2: P2, *K2, P2* rep from * to * to end.
Rep these 2 rows until rib meas 4 cm (1½ ins), ending after a rs row.
Next Row (ws): Rib 7(13, 7), *M1, rib 10* rep from * to * to last 7(13, 7) sts, M1, rib to end. (147(159, 169) sts)
Change to 3.25 mm (No. 10) needles and cont in st.st, starting with a K row. Work rows 1–72 of chart, starting and finishing where indicated for sizes. Rep these 72 rows until Back meas 33(34, 36) cm (13(13½, 14) ins) from beg, ending after a ws row.

Shape armholes
Keeping patt correct throughout, cast off 8(9, 9) sts at beg of next 2 rows. Now dec one st at each end of foll 6 rows, then on every foll alt row to 111(119, 127) sts.**
Cont straight until Back meas (55(56, 59) cm (21½(22, 23) ins) from beg, ending after a ws row.

Shape Neck
Keeping patt correct, cont thus:
Next Row (rs): Patt 37(40, 43) sts, TURN.
*** Cont on these sts only and dec one st at neck edge on next 2 rows.
Work one row straight. Cast off rem 35(38, 41) sts.
Slip 37(39, 41) sts centre back on to st-holder for back neck.
Rejoin yarn at neck edge of rem 37(40, 43) sts, and work one row straight.
Complete as for first side of neck from *** to end.

FRONT

Work as given for Back to **.
Cont straight until Front meas 47(48, 50) cm (18½(19, 19½) ins) from beg, ending after a ws row.

Shape Neck
Keeping patt correct, cont thus:
Next Row (rs): Patt 48(51, 55) sts, TURN.

/ = Col A (Pale Blue)
□ = Col B (White)
○ = Col C (Green)
^ = Col D (Pink)
● = Col E (Yellow)
X = Col F (Peach)
• = Col G (Turquoise)

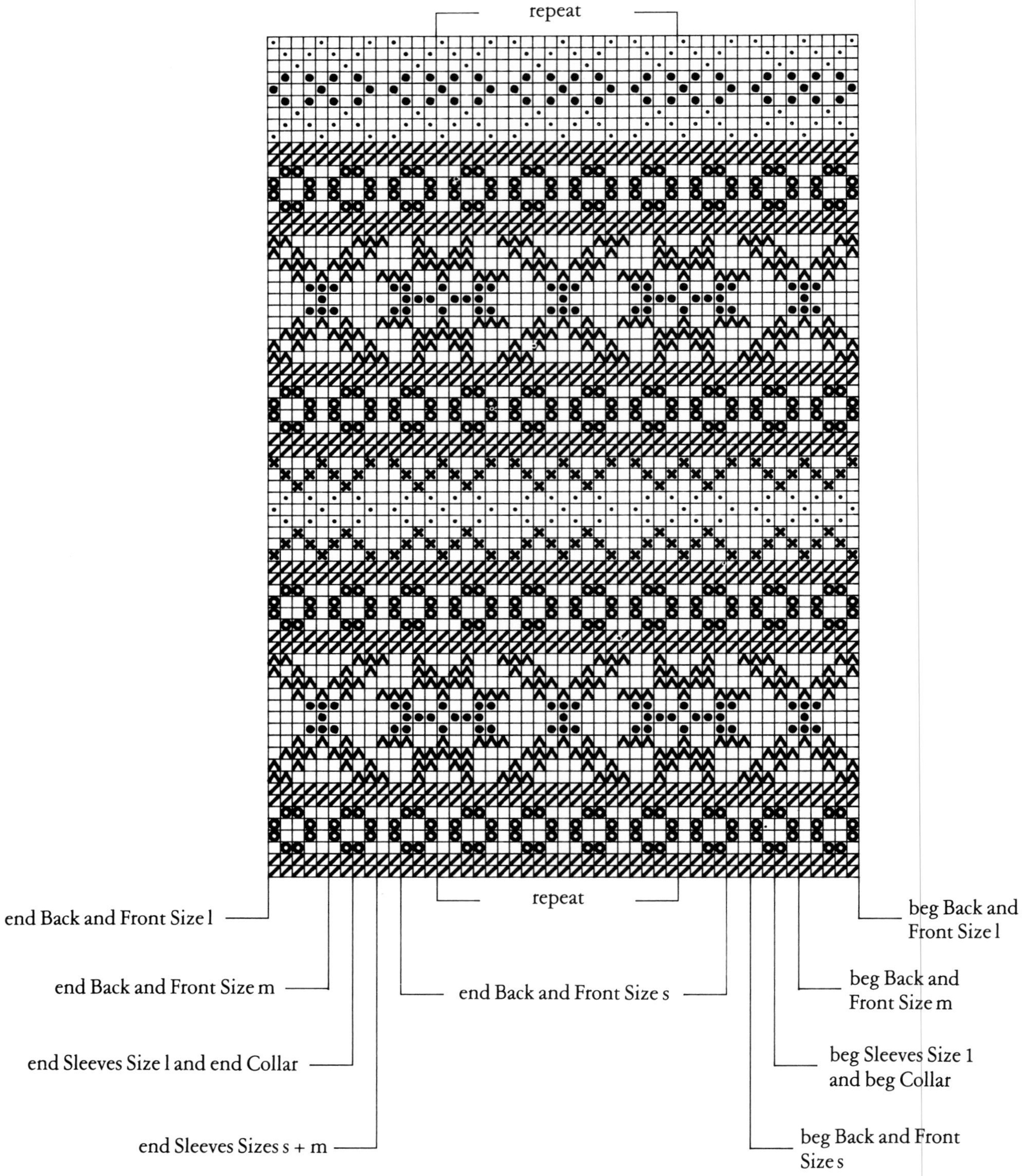

repeat

repeat

end Back and Front Size l

end Back and Front Size m

end Sleeves Size l and end Collar

end Sleeves Sizes s + m

end Back and Front Size s

beg Back and Front Size l

beg Back and Front Size m

beg Sleeves Size 1 and beg Collar

beg Back and Front Size s

****Cont on these sts only and dec one st at neck edge on next 6 rows, then on every foll alt row to 35(38, 41) sts. Cont straight until Front matches Back to shoulder. Cast off.
Slip 15(17, 17) sts centre front on to st-holder for front neck.
Rejoin yarn at neck edge of rem 48(51, 55) sts, and work one row straight.
Complete as given for first side of neck from **** to end.

SLEEVES

With 2.75 mm (No. 12) needles and A, cast on 54(54, 58) sts, and work 4 cm (1½ ins) of K2, P2 rib as given for Back, ending after a rs row.
Next Row (ws): Rib 3(3, 5), *M1, rib 3* rep from * to * to last 3(3, 5) sts, M1, rib to end. (71(71, 75) sts)
Change to 3.25 mm (No. 10) needles and cont in st.st, starting with a K row. Beg at rows 45(49, 49), then rep the 72 rows as set work chart, starting and finishing where indicated for sizes, AT THE SAME TIME inc one st at each end of 9th row and every foll 4th row until there are 101(101, 105) sts, then every 6th row to 115(117, 121) sts, working extra sts into patt. Cont straight until sleeve meas approx 41(41, 42.5) cm (16(16, 16¾ ins) from beg, ending after a ws row, and finishing with same patt row as Back and Front before armhole shaping.

Shape Top
Keeping patt correct, cast off 8(9, 9) sts at beg of next 2 rows, then dec one st at each end of foll 16(16, 18) rows. (67 sts)
Work 10 rows straight, then dec one st at each end of next row and foll 3 alt rows. (59 sts)
Cast off 2 sts at beg of next 6 rows, 4 sts at beg of next 6 rows, then 6 sts at beg of foll 2 rows. Cast off rem 11 sts.

NECKBAND

Sew right shoulder seam.
With 2.75 mm (No. 12) needles and A, and with rs facing, pick up and K33(33, 36) sts evenly down left front neck shaping, K15(17, 17) sts from st-holder centre front, pick up and K33(33, 36) sts evenly up right front neck shaping, pick up and K4 sts down right back neck shaping, K37(39, 41) sts from st-holder centre back, and pick up and K4 sts up left back neck shaping. (126(130, 138) sts)
Beg with row 2, work 2 cm (¾in) of K2, P2 rib as given for Back. Cast off ribwise.

COLLAR

With 3.25 mm (No. 10) needles and A, cast on 155 sts, and K5 rows. (garter st)
Cont in st.st, starting with a K row, and work rows 9–26 of chart, beg and ending where indicated.
With A, cont thus:
Next Row (rs): K1(5, 10), *K2 tog, K2* rep from * to * to last 2(6, 13) sts, K2 tog, K0(4, 11). (116(118, 121) sts)
Beg with a P row, work 5 rows st.st. Cast off.
With 3.25 mm (No. 10) needles and A, and with rs facing, pick up and K25 sts up right selvedge of collar, and work 2 rows garter st. Cast off.
With 3.25 mm (No. 10) needles and A, and with rs facing, pick up and K25 sts down left selvedge of collar, and work 2 rows garter st. Cast off.

TO MAKE UP

Weave in all loose ends. Sew left shoulder and neckband seam. Sew sleeves into position, matching cast-off sts underarm. Sew side and sleeve seams. With opening centre front, sew ws of cast-off edge of collar to ws of pick-up row of neckband. Fold collar to rs over top of neckband.

LADIES' BOXY CREW-NECK SWEATER (HAND KNIT)

SIZES

	small	*medium*	*large*	
To fit bust:	86–91 34–36	97–102 38–40	107–112 42–44	cm ins
Actual bust measurement:	97 38	107 42	117 46	cm ins
Length:	54 21¼	56 22	59 23¼	cm ins
Sleeve (seam):	41 16	42 16½	43 17	cm ins

MATERIALS

Jamieson Spinning 4-ply Wool (50 grm balls)

Col A	200	200	200 grms	(Green)
Col B	100	100	100 grms	(Brown)
Col C	100	100	100 grms	(White)
Col D	50	50	100 grms	(Pink)
Col E	100	100	100 grms	(Yellow)
Col F	50	50	50 grms	(Blue)

1 pair each size 2.75 mm (No. 12) and 3.25 mm (No. 10) knitting needles.
Stitch holders.

TENSION

30 sts and 33 rows to 10 cm (4 ins) over patt using 3.25 mm (No. 10) needles.

ABBREVIATIONS

K – Knit; P – Purl; st(s) – stitch(es); st.st – stocking stitch; alt – alternate; beg – beginning; cont – continue; foll – following; inc – increase; dec – decrease; meas – measures; M1 – make one stich by picking up, twisting and knitting bar between stitches; patt – pattern; rem – remaining; rep – repeat; rs – right side; ws – wrong side.

NOTES

Read chart by reading rs rows from right to left, and ws rows from left to right, and starting and finishing where indicated for sizes and sections.

When carrying yarn over less than 6 sts, do not weave carrying colours into fabric. Place the carrying yarns along the ws of fabric, taking care to leave sufficient length of yarn so as not to pucker the fabric. When carrying over 6 sts or more, catch carrying yarn once in middle of carry.

BACK

With 2.75 mm (No. 12) needles and A, cast on 134(146, 158) sts.
Row 1 (rs): K2, *P2, K2* rep from * to * to end.
Row 2: P2, *K2, P2* rep from * to * to end.
Rep these 2 rows until rib meas 2.5 cm (1 in), ending after a rs row.
Next Row (ws): Rib 7(3, 7), *M1, rib 10(10, 8)* rep from * to * to last 7(3, 7) sts, M1, rib to end. (147(161, 177) sts)
Change to 3.25 mm (No. 10) needles and cont in st. st, starting with a K row. Work rows 1–34 of chart, starting and finishing where indicated for sizes. Rep these 34 rows until Back meas 53(55, 58) cm (20¾(21½, 22¾) ins) from beg, ending after a ws row.

Shape Neck
Keeping patt correct, cont thus:
Next Row (rs): Patt 56(62, 69) sts, TURN.
** Cont on these sts only and dec one st at neck edge of next 2 rows.
Work one row straight. Cast off rem 54(60, 67) sts.
Slip 35(37, 39) sts centre back on to st-holder for back neck.
Rejoin yarn at neck edge of rem 56(62, 69) sts and work one row straight. Complete as given for first side of neck from ** to end.

FRONT

Work as given for Back until Front meas 46(48, 50) cm (18(18¾, 19¾) ins) from beg, ending after a ws row.

Shape Neck
Keeping patt correct, cont thus:
Next Row (rs): Patt 65(72, 79) sts, TURN.
***Cont on these sts only and dec one st at neck edge on next 8 rows, then on every foll alt row to 54(60, 67) sts. Cont straight until Front matches Back to shoulder. Cast off.
Slip 17(17, 19) sts centre front on to st-holder.
Rejoin yarn at neck edge of rem 65(72, 79) sts and work one row straight. Complete as given for first side of neck from *** to end.

SLEEVES

With 2.75 mm (No. 12) needles and A, cast on 54(58, 62) sts and work 2.5 cm (1 in) of K2, P2 rib as given for Back, ending after a rs row.
Next Row (ws): Rib 3(5, 4), *M1, rib 3* rep from * to * to last 3(5, 4) sts,

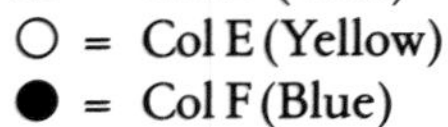
□ = Col A (Green)
• = Col B (Brown)
/ = Col C (White)
X = Col D (Pink)
○ = Col E (Yellow)
● = Col F (Blue)

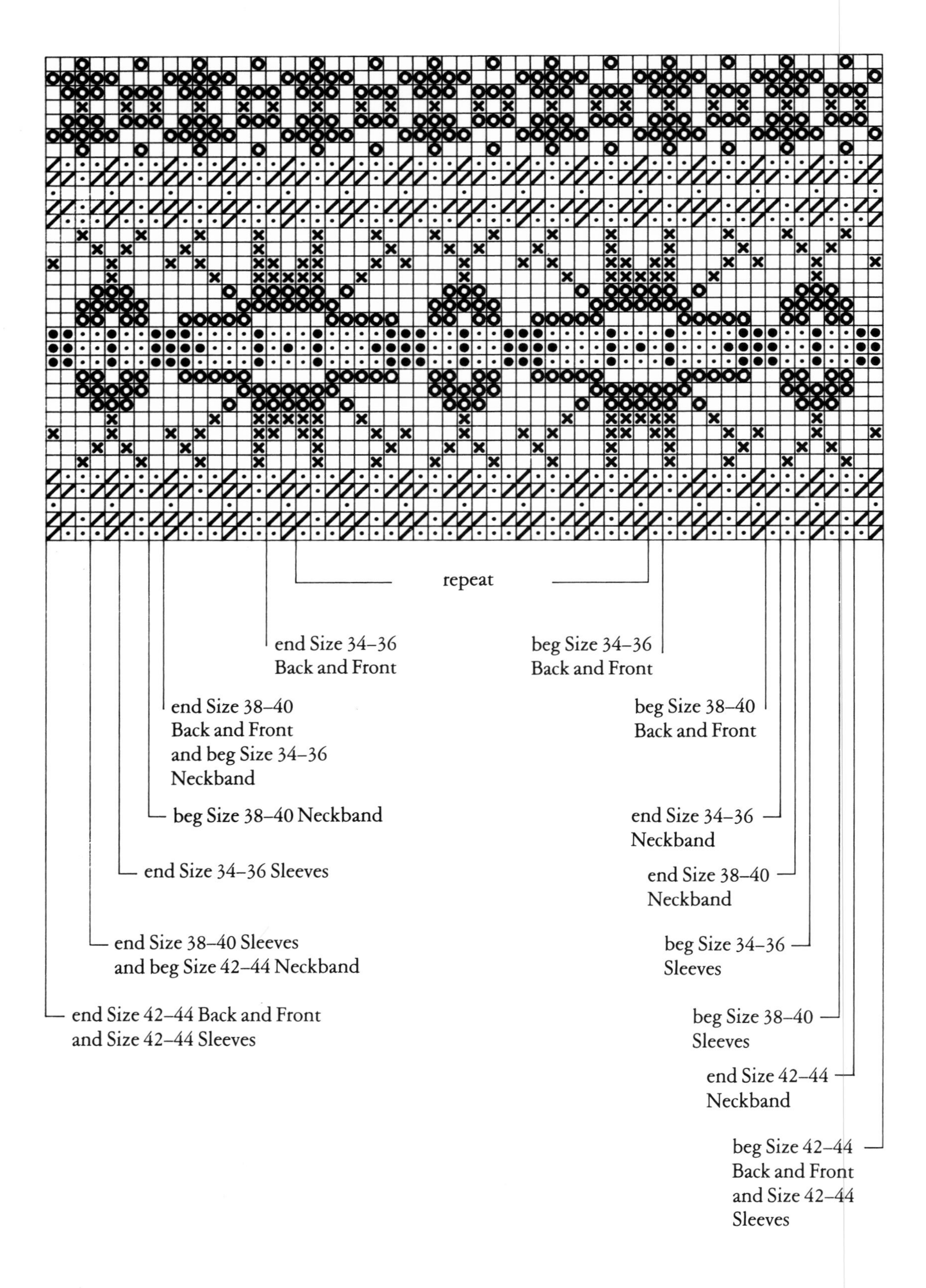
repeat
end Size 34–36 Back and Front
beg Size 34–36 Back and Front
end Size 38–40 Back and Front and beg Size 34–36 Neckband
beg Size 38–40 Back and Front
beg Size 38–40 Neckband
end Size 34–36 Neckband
end Size 34–36 Sleeves
end Size 38–40 Neckband
end Size 38–40 Sleeves and beg Size 42–44 Neckband
beg Size 34–36 Sleeves
end Size 42–44 Back and Front and Size 42–44 Sleeves
beg Size 38–40 Sleeves
end Size 42–44 Neckband
beg Size 42–44 Back and Front and Size 42–44 Sleeves

M1, rib to end. (71(75, 81) sts)
Change to 3.25 mm (No. 10) needles and st. st, starting with a K row.
Work rows 1–34 of chart, starting and finishing where indicated, then rep chart as required, AT THE SAME TIME inc one st at each end of 9th row and every foll 4th row to 89(107, 133) sts, then every foll 6th row to 113(125, 137) sts, working extra sts into patt. Cont straight until sleeve meas 41(42, 43) cm (16(16½, 17) ins) from beg, ending after a ws row.
Cast off loosely.

NECKBAND

Sew right shoulder seam.
With 3.25 mm (No. 10) needles and A, and with rs facing, pick up and K28(28, 30) sts evenly down left front neck shaping, K17(17, 19) sts from st-holder centre front, pick up and K28(28, 30) sts evenly up right front neck shaping, pick up and K3 sts down right back neck shaping, K35(37, 39) sts from st-holder centre back, and pick up and K3 sts up left back neck shaping. (114(116, 124) sts)
Cont in st.st, STARTING WITH A P ROW, and work rows 1–5 of chart.
Change to 2.75 mm (No. 12) needles and work 6 rows st.st with A.
Using 3.25 mm (No. 10) needles, cast off loosely.

TO MAKE UP

Weave in all loose ends. Sew left shoulder and neckband seam. Fold neckband in half to ws and sew down. Beg and ending 19(21, 22.5) cm (7½(8¼, 9) ins) down side edges from shoulder seams, sew sleeves to sides. Sew side and sleeve seams.

Machine Knitting

MAN'S CLASSIC CREW-NECK SWEATER (MACHINE KNIT)

SIZES

To fit chest:	114 cm 46 ins
Length	65 cm 26 ins
Sleeve (centre body to cuff):	80 cm 32 ins

MATERIALS

Jamieson 4-ply Wool

Col A	220 grms	(Navy)
Col B	30 grms	(Rust)
Col C	40 grms	(Fawn)
Col D	55 grms	(Natural)
Col E	20 grms	(Camel)
Col F	220 grms	(Blue)

TENSION

15 sts and 16 rows to 5 cm (2 ins) over patt.

NOTES

Punchcard must be made exactly as chart so that sweater will match at side seams.

BACK

Using ribbing attachment, cast on 156 stitches.
Knit 41 rows.
Push 85 needles into working position to left of 0 and 84 to right side.
Set punchcard to row 1. Transfer stitches from ribber on to needles increasing 1 stitch every 12 needles to increase 13 stitches across bed.
Knit 107 rows.
Insert marker (a piece of thread on end needles) for start of sleeve. Knit to row 192. Knit off on waste yarn.

FRONT

Knit as back to row 157.
Take 24 stitches at left side of 0 and 23 at right side of machine on to a

thread. Put 47 needles out of work. Put needles at left side to non-working position.
Knit right side, decreasing 1 stitch every two rows five times at neck edge, then knit straight to row 192.
Knit off on waste yarn.
Reset punchcard and knit left side to match.

Hand graft shoulder seams in main colour and Swiss with contrast colour darn so pattern matches.

SLEEVES

Using main colour, knit up stitches (one for each row) between sleeve markers.
Push 87 needles to left side of 0 and 86 to right side into working position. Set punchcard to row 1. Transfer sleeve stitches to needles.
Decrease 1 stitch every two rows nine times then 1 stitch every four rows to row 157. (91 stitches)
Knit off on waste yarn.

CUFFS

Using ribbing attachment cast on 80 stitches.
Knit 36 rows.

NECK

Using ribbing attachment cast on 160 stitches.
Knit 34 rows.

FINISHING OFF

Hand graft cuffs to sleeves decreasing evenly across the sleeve to lose 11 stitches to match cuff.
To finish double crew neck:
Using main colour, pick up 35 stitches from right side of neck, 47 stitches from front, 35 stitches from left side of neck and 57 stitches from neck.
Hand graft neck rib to stitches from neck, decreasing evenly 5 stitches on each side and 4 on back.
Sew side seam of neck, fold rib double and stitch down to inside.
Using double thread sew side seam and sleeve seam through centre of edge stitch of work. Finish threads by passing through seam and looping through back of work. This not only gets rid of loose ends but also tightens up seam to correct tension. Finish off ends around sleeve join and neck edge by looping through back of work.

□ = Col A (Navy)
/ = Col B (Rust)
○ = Col C (Fawn)
• = Col D (Natural)
X = Col E (Camel)
■ = Col F (Blue)

Row 1

LADIES' CLASSIC CARDIGAN IN BUTTON-THROUGH STYLE (MACHINE KNIT)

SIZES

To fit chest:	105 cm 42 ins
Length:	60 cm 24 ins
Sleeve (centre body to cuff):	75 cm 30 ins

MATERIALS

Laidlaw and Fairgrieve or Nethy Products 4-ply wool

Col A	260 grms	(Myrtle)
Col B	120 grms	(Bilberry)
Col C	15 grms	(Cedarwood)
Col D	10 grms	(Shellduck)
Col E	50 grms	(Rosso Red)
Col F	50 grms	(Rowan)
Col G	35 grms	(Forest Green)
Col H	35 grms	(Tale)

TENSION

15 sts and 16 rows to 5 cm (2 ins) over patt.

NOTES

The punchcard must be made exactly as the chart so that the sweater will match at side seams. Shoulder seams are slightly set back to allow for grafting on a plain row and continuity of pattern.

BACK

Using ribbing attachment, cast on 132 stitches.
Knit 41 rows.
Push 73 needles into working position to left side of 0 and 72 to right side. Set punchcard to row 1. Transfer stitches from rib on to needles, increasing 1 stitch every 10 to increase 13 stitches across bed. Knit 103 rows.
Take 16 stitches from each side of work off machine on to a thread. Take 16 needles at each side out of work.
Decrease 1 stitch every two rows six times on each side. Knit to row 166.
Knit off on waste yarn.

LEFT FRONT

Using ribbing attachment, cast on 66 stitches.
Knit 41 rows.
Push 49 needles into working position to left of 0 and 24 to right side.
Set punchcard to row 1. Transfer stitches from rib on to needles, increasing 1 stitch every 9 to increase 7 stitches across bed. Knit 103 rows.
Take 16 stitches from left side of work off machine on to a thread. Take 16 needles out of work.
Decrease 1 stitch every two rows six times on left side. Knit to row 143.
Take 22 stitches from right side of work off machine on to a thread. Take 22 needles out of work.
Decrease 1 stitch every two rows five times at right side. Knit to row 176.
Knit off on waste yarn.

RIGHT FRONT

Using ribbing attachment, cast on 66 stitches.
Knit 41 rows.
Push 25 needles into working position to left of 0 and 48 to right side.
Set punchcard to row 1. Transfer stitches from rib onto needles, increasing 1 stitch every 9 to increase 7 stitches across bed. Knit 103 rows.
Take 16 stitches from right side of work off machine on to a thread. Take 16 needles out of work.
Decrease 1 stitch every two rows six times on right side. Knit to row 143.
Take 22 stitches from left side of work off machine on to a thread. Take 22 needles out of work.
Decrease 1 stitch every two rows five times at left side. Knit to row 176.
Knit off on waste yarn.
Hand graft shoulder seams.

SLEEVES

Pick up 16 stitches from each side of work, knit up 137 stitches from sleeve edge (one for each row). (169 stitches)
Push 81 needles into working position to left of 0 and 80 to right side.
Set punchcard to row 17. Transfer stitches to needles, decreasing 1 stitch every 20 to lose 8 stitches across bed.
Decrease 1 stitch every two rows eight times then knit evenly to row 136 then knit to row 151. (85 stitches)
Knit off on waste yarn.

CUFFS

Using ribbing attachment cast on 72 stitches.
Knit 51 rows.

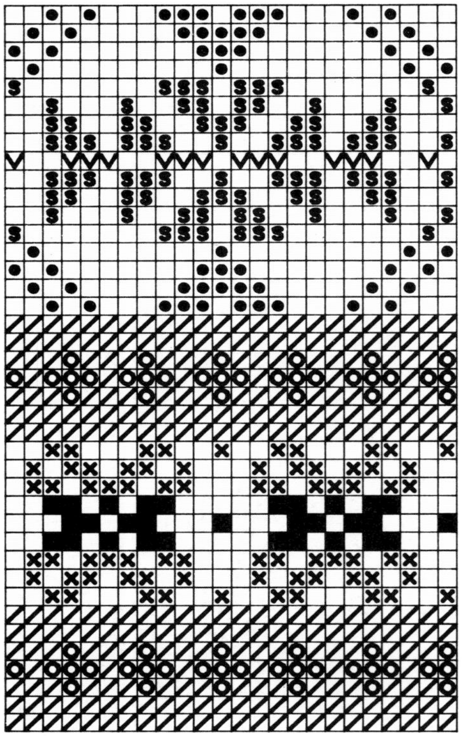

Row 1

☐ = Col A (Myrtle)
/ = Col B (Bilberry)
■ = Col C (Cedarwood)
V = Col D (Shellduck)
• = Col E (Rosso Red)
S = Col F (Rowan)
X = Col G (Forest Green)
○ = Col H (Tale)

NECK

Using ribbing attachment cast on 160 stitches.
Knit 42 rows.

RIGHT FRONT FACING

Using ribbing attachment cast on 22 stitches. Knit 6 rows.
Make 10 buttonholes, 25 rows between each. Knit 6 rows. Cast off. (237 rows)

LEFT FRONT FACING

Cast on 22 stitches.
Knit 237 rows.
Cast off.

FINISHING OFF

Hand graft cuffs to sleeves decreasing evenly across the sleeve to lose 13 stitches to match cuff.
To finish double crew neck:
Using main colour, pick up 22 stitches from each side of work, 33 stitches from right side of neck, 51 from back neck, 33 stitches from left side. Hand graft neck rib to stitches from neck. Fold rib double and stitch down to inside.
Using double thread sew side seam and sleeve seam through centre of edge stitch of work. Finish threads by passing through seam and looping through back of work. This not only gets rid of loose ends but also tightens up seam to correct tension. Finish threads around sleeve join and neck edges by looping through back of work. Sew on facings using mattress stitch. Stretch facing slightly to fit front edge. Finish loose threads by looping through back of work.

MAN'S WAISTCOAT WITH POCKETS (MACHINE KNIT)

SIZES

To fit chest:	114 cm 46 ins
Length	62.5 cm 25 ins

MATERIALS

Jamieson & Smith 4-ply wool

Col A	35 grms	(Peach)
Col B	65 grms	(Rust)
Col C	65 grms	(Rich Cream)
Col D	170 grms	(Blue)
Col E	65 grms	(Dark Green)
Col F	65 grms	(White)

TENSION

15 sts and 16 rows to 5 cm (2 ins) over patt.

NOTES

The punchcard must be made exactly as the chart so that the sweater will match at side seams. Shoulder seams are slightly set back, this is to allow for grafting on a plain row and continuity of pattern.

BACK

Using ribbing attachment, cast on 156 stitches.
Knit 41 rows.
Push 85 needles into working position to left of 0 and 84 to right side.
Set punchcard to row 1. Transfer stitches from rib on to needles increasing 1 stitch every 12 to increase 13 stitches across bed. Knit 109 rows.
Take 17 stitches from each side of work off machine on to a thread. Take 17 needles at each side out of work.
Decrease 1 stitch every two rows eight times on each side. Knit to row 187.
Knit off on waste yarn.

• = Col A (Peach)
○ = Col B (Rust)
X = Col C (Rich Cream)
□ = Col D (Blue)
/ = Col E (Dark Green)
■ = Col F (White)

POCKET LININGS

Using one tension tighter than main tension, knit 36 rows over 36 needles plain knitting. Knit two pieces and knit off on waste yarn.

LEFT FRONT

Using ribbing attachment, cast on 78 stitches.
Knit 41 rows.
Push 37 needles into working position to left of 0 and 48 to right side.
Set punchcard to row 1. Transfer stitches from rib on to needles increasing 1 stitch every 10 to increase 8 stitches across bed. Knit 36 rows.
Select 12 stitches to left of 0 and 24 to right side. Take the stitches off the needles on to a thread (those 36 stitches are the top of pocket). With wrong side of pocket lining facing, transfer 36 stitches from top of lining to empty needles. Knit to row 83.
Start decreasing 1 stitch every 4 rows on right side only. Knit to row 109.
Take 17 stitches from left side of work off machine onto a thread. Take 17 needles at left side out of work.

While decreasing on right side, decrease 1 stitch every two rows eight times on left side. Continue to decrease on right side 1 stitch every four rows. Knit to row 198.
Knit off on waste yarn.

RIGHT FRONT

Make rib as for left front. Push 49 needles into working position to left of 0 and 36 to right. Knit as left front to row 36.
Select 25 stitches to left of 0 and 11 to right side. Take the stitches off the needles onto a thread. With wrong side of pocket lining facing transfer 36 stitches from lining to empty needles. Knit to row 83.
Start decreasing 1 stitch every 4 rows on left side only. Knit to row 109.
Take 17 stitches from right side of work off machine onto a thread. Take 17 needles at right side out of work.
While decreasing on left side, decrease 1 stitch every two rows eight times on right side. Continue to decrease 1 stitch on left side every four rows. Knit to row 198.
Knit off on waste yarn.
Hand graft shoulder seams and cast off stitches at back neck.

POCKET RIB

Using ribber attachment, cast on 36 stitches.
Knit 15 rows.
Knit two pieces.

ARMBAND

Using ribber attachment, cast on 200 stitches.
Knit 15 rows.
Knit two pieces.

FACING

Using ribber attachment, cast on 16 stitches.
Knit 6 rows.
Make six buttonholes with 22 rows between each. Knit 620 rows.
Cast off.

FINISHING OFF

To attach armband, pick up 17 stitches from each side of work and using main colour knit up 166 stitches (one for each row). Hand graft rib stitches to 200 stitches from garment. Finish off loose ends by looping through back of work.
Hand graft rib to top of pocket and stitch down edges of rib. Stitch pocket linings in place and finish off loose threads.
Join side seams using double thread, sew through centre of edge stitch of work. Finish threads by passing through seam and looping through back of work. This not only gets rid of loose ends but also tightens up seam to correct tension.
Sew on facing using mattress seam. Stretch facing slightly to fit front edge. Finish off loose ends by looping through back of work.

YARN SUPPLIERS

All the sweaters with the exception of the Unisex Vee-Neck, were knitted in 4-ply yarns and all the companies listed supply good colour ranges in this quality. The vee-neck sweater was worked in Double Knitting yarn from Rowan Yarns

T M Hunter Ltd
Bora
Sutherland
Scotland
Tel: 040 831 366

Jamieson & Smith Ltd
90 North Road
Lerwick
Shetland
Scotland ZE1 0PQ
Tel: 0595 3579

Jamieson Spinning Ltd
Sandness Industrial Estate
Sandness
Shetland ZE1 9TI
Tel: 0595 87 285

Laidlaw & Fairgrieve Ltd
Riverside Mill
Selkirk
Selkirkshire
Scotland TD7 5EF
Tel: 0750 2065

Nethy Products
Kirkshaw Road
Coatbridge
Scotland ML5 5SL
Tel: 0236 40484

Rowan Yarns
Green Lane Mill
Holmefirth
Huddersfield
West Yorkshire
HD7 1RW
Tel: 0484 681881

Pamela Wise
101–105 Groswell Road
London EC1V 7ER
Tel: 071 490 0037

Sweaters from the designs illustrated in Chapter 5 and the machine knitted garment patterns can be obtained from:

Shetland Designer
Swarthoull
Cunningsburgh
Shetland ZE2 9HB
Tel: 095 03 257

A mail order catalogue of traditional and classic Shetland knitwear is available from:

Shetland Knitwear Trades Association
175a Commercial Street
Lerwick
Shetland ZE1 0JL
Tel: 0595 5631

BIBLIOGRAPHY

Helen Bennett, *Scottish Knitting*, (Shire Publications, 1986)
Rae Compton, *Complete Book of Traditional Knitting*, (Batsford, 1983)
Sara Don, *Fair Isle Knitting*, (Bell & Hyman, 1984)
James W Irvine, *Lerwick*, (Lerwick Community Council, 1985)
Sheila McGregor, *The Complete Book of Traditional Scandinavian Knitting*, (Batsford, 1984)
Sheila McGregor, *Traditional Knitting*, (Batsford, 1983)
Gwyn Morgan, *Traditional Knitting Patterns in the British Isles*, (Ward Lock, 1981)
James R Nicholson, *Lerwick Harbour*, (Lerwick Harbour Trust, 1977)
James R Nicholson, *Shetland*, (David & Charles, 1984)
James R Nicholson, *Shetland Folklore*, (Hale, 1981)
James Norbury, *Traditional Knitting Patterns from Scandinavia, the British Isles, France, Italy and other European Countries*, (Dover Publications, 1984)
Michael Pearson, *Traditional Knitting*, (Collins, 1983)
Alice Starmore, *Fair Isle Knitting*, (Taunton Books & Videos, 1988)
Lizbeth Upitis, *Latvian Mittens, Traditional Designs and Techniques*, (Dos Tejedoras, 1981 – distributed by Alison Hodge, Cornwall)
Madeline Weston, *The Traditional Knitting Book*, (Dorling Kindersley, 1986)